The *Faith and Life* series is a contemporary approach to adult religious education. It treats major areas of Christian concern: the roots of Christianity in the Bible and worship; the meaning of God, Christ, and the Church in a pluralistic culture; the place of prayer and Christian example in a secular age.

The intent of the authors and editors is that books of the *Faith and Life* series will provoke lively discussion about the relevance of religion, and lead to deeper understanding of what it means to be a Christian in the world of today.

Contributing authors represent an interfaith spectrum of viewpoints, including Baptist, Catholic, Lutheran, and Presbyterian. Each book in the series is a complete subject for study and discussion, presenting its own topics, references, and bibliographies.

General editors of the *Faith and Life* series are two Catholic priests—Francis Buckley, S.J., and Cyr M̲ Miller, with wide experience in religious educa

D1247623

Books in the FAITH AND LIFE series

Christian Decision and Action by Albert R. Jonsen

Christians of Vision and Venture: Profiles in Spiritual Courage by Toivo K. I. Harjunpaa

Christianity and War: Religious Ideas and Political Consequences by Leonard J. Weber

The Church: Its Credibility Today by James P. Mackey

The God Who Loves by A. Durwood Foster

Is It Too Late? A Theology of Ecology by John B. Cobb, Jr.

The Man for Others by Ben F. Meyer

Marriage and Sex: A Christian Perspective by Charles P. Kindregan

Men of Prayer, Men of Action: Christian Spirituality Today by Barnabas M. Ahern

Worship and Witness by C. J. McNaspy

An excellent guide to the establishment of adult religious education programs is *Christians Are Not for Lions: Adult Religious Education Today* by Cyr N. Miller (New York: 1971).

Is It Too Late?

A Theology of Ecology

JOHN B. COBB, JR.

Bruce/Beverly Hills, California

Contents

Preface

Public awareness of the ecological crisis may increasingly dominate our cultural climate in the 1970s. Indeed, if it does not do so, there is little chance that measures needed for the survival of civilization will be taken in time. If the awareness does grow, it will seriously challenge us as Christians to rethink our faith.

Such rethinking will be neither comfortable nor easy. Our most fundamental picture of ourselves as human beings in relation to God and to a subhuman environment will be at stake.

This book represents one Christian's response to this new questioning. I am led by my questioning to believe that the major forms of past Christianity are inadequate to our needs and must be superseded. But I have also concluded that it is fruitless to seek the vision we need in primitive or Oriental religions. Our task is instead to move forward to a new form of Christianity.

Obviously my idea of a new form of Christianity is only mine. It has no authority except its intrinsic merit. Some Christians will disagree that basic change is required. Others will disagree as to the appropriate direction of change. My hope is, not to persuade all Christians to accept my conclusions, but to help to stimulate reconsideration of widespread attitudes and to encourage a debate that takes seriously the threat of doom under which we now live.

PART ONE

The Need for a New Vision

I

What's the Problem?

The great question of the seventies is: shall we . . .
begin to make reparations for the damage we have
done to our air, to our land and to our water?

Richard M. Nixon
"State of the Union Message," 1970

Simple arithmetic yields astounding results. It
shows that beginning with a hundred dollars you only
have to double your money ten times in order to have
a hundred thousand dollars. If you double it ten more
times, you would have a hundred million dollars.
Since most of us could raise a hundred dollars, this is
very encouraging. It seems to make wealth more accessible than we ordinarily think.

But the same rate of growth applies in other areas
where the results are frightening. For example, if the
world population continues to double about three
times a century, by 2300 it will have increased one
thousand fold, and by 2633 it will have increased one
million fold. In 2300 there will be three and a half
trillion people, and in 2633 there will be 3,500,-
000,000,000,000. The latter figure is too much for
our imagination. The former is bad enough. In fact,
one thing of which we can be certain is that there
really won't be three and a half trillion people in
2300. Can you imagine Japan with one hundred bil-

lion people, that is, thirty times the present population of the whole planet? Or can you imagine China
with eight hundred billion, or even this country with
two hundred billion? No, that is all quite impossible.
Something will happen to prevent it.

When driving across vast barren stretches of the
American West, one might recall that once great herds
of buffalo found tall grass growing there. We know
that we slaughtered the buffalo, but we ask what has
happened to the grass. Sometimes the answer is that
sheep were brought in and in a few years brambles
took over. Sometimes we learn that wells were drilled
and the water table lowered. But there were other,
more favored lands to which men could move.

For some years those of us who live in Southern
California have been complaining about the smog. It
stings the eyes, aggravates the sinuses, reduces the grape
harvest, and hides the beauty of the mountains from
our view. We have been told that it is the result of
local problems of atmospheric inversion and that
stricter controls will take care of it.

From time to time an old swimming hole or a
once fashionable beach is closed. The sanitation de-
partment tells us it is no longer suitable for swimming. But we can build fine new swimming pools and
fill them with chemically purified water. Streams and
pools in which we once fished are now dead, but with
our superior transportation we can go higher into the
mountains to catch fish supplied to those lakes and
streams by our public hatcheries.

In 1966 the East coast suffered a spectacular
blackout because of an electrical power failure. Less
publicized failures are not infrequent occurrences. But
more generating plants can be built, and the electrical
grid of the nation can be interconnected.

The last dodo died in 1689, and a hundred more
species of birds have since vanished forever. But there

are plenty of other birds. The California grizzly is extinct, but there are plenty of other bears. The giant Galápagos turtle will soon be gone from its native home, but the San Diego Zoo will preserve the species.

Both the United States and the Soviet Union have enough atomic weapons to destroy all humanity several times over. Their arsenals of chemical and bacteriological warfare are no less potent. But they exercise restraint.

One out of every four persons born today will carry through life the irreversible physical or psychological effects of malnutrition. Thousands starve every day. Protein deficiency stunts the normal development of intelligence. We are assured that agricultural technology will solve these problems.

Insect pests develop new strains capable of surviving chemical insecticides, while their natural enemies, the birds, are killed. We undertake to control the use of such insecticides while raising the official level of allowable contamination in milk and poultry.

For some time we have been more or less aware of one or more of these matters. We have felt some sadness, even a little anger, but we have accepted them as the price of progress. If the situation ever became really serious, we assure ourselves, our leaders would correct it.

It is only quite recently that we have begun to realize that all these problems are interconnected and cumulative. The attempt to solve one problem all too often worsens others. Furthermore, they are neither local nor temporary. The transformation of forests and grasslands into brambles and dustbowls has been going on for thousands of years. Ancient civilizations collapsed when they destroyed their agricultural base, but these were *local* problems. Now civilization is worldwide, and if our worldwide resources in soil are further depleted, there will be nowhere left to turn.

Smog may be an especially severe problem in the Los Angeles basin because of atmospheric inversion, but it is now a national and worldwide problem as well. The smog of Tokyo is breathed in California. It is not the air here and there, but the total planetary atmosphere that is being poisoned.

It is no longer just an occasional stream that has been turned into a sewer. Most of our major waterways are seriously polluted. Lake Erie is dead and Lake Michigan is fast dying. Even Lake Tahoe is affected! When Paul Ehrlich wrote a science fiction scenario entitled *The Year the Oceans Died,* projecting present trends, his date was not 2300 but 1979!

The problem of an adequate supply of electrical power is proving to be nationwide. Good sites for more dams are becoming scarce. The public is alerted to the risks of atomic power. The use of coal and oil pollutes the air and hastens the depletion of these resources.

Whereas species of birds and animals have become extinct throughout history, the rate is increasing rapidly. From A.D. 1 to 1800 one species of mammal was exterminated each 55 years. In this century the rate of extinction is one per year. Today the threat to their survival is wholesale. In some instances they are decimated by more efficient and ruthless methods of hunting. In others their ancient habitats are taken over by man. In still others their environment or their food is poisoned. Rachel Carson foresees a "silent spring" when birds will sing no more.

The United States and the Soviet Union may continue to exercise restraint in the employment of their ultimate weapons, but more and more countries are gaining possession of them. Even if these resist the temptation to use them, danger remains. The problem of storage and disposal of radioactive wastes has not been solved, and we dump outdated bacteriological weapons into the ocean on the untested assumption that the water will sufficiently dilute their virulence to prevent major damage.

Although we are making a little progress in controlling the use of DDT, we must remember that great quantities are already lying around in our soil and water, finding their way up the food chain to us, and being carried through the rivers to the continental shelves. We must watch helplessly as they do their work of damage both in our own bodies and in the minute marine life that is the basis for the food chain in the ocean. Virtually all of California's oceanic bird-life is already doomed. Meanwhile, our chemical industry continues to produce new products whose effects upon our environment are unknown. And while we are beginning to be more careful with our insecticides and weed poisons, the pressure of population on the food supply of the underdeveloped world greatly increases the demand for dangerous chemicals there.

At the moment, newly developed high yield grains are bringing about a "green revolution." Perhaps India will be able to feed its present population after all. This is cause for great rejoicing. But the risks, too, are great. The new strains of grain may prove subject to as yet unknown pests and diseases to which the native strains were resistant. The tragedy of the Irish in the last century points up the danger. There the whole national agriculture shifted to potatoes because of the quantity that could be grown. The population of the island multiplied. Then came the potato blight. Millions starved and other millions emigrated to save their lives. If the "green revolution" encourages the upward spiraling of India's already vast population, the result of a blight could be disastrous indeed! The present corn blight in this country reminds us that even *our* scientific and technological skills are sometimes impotent.

We are being made to realize that the problem of

overpopulation is not one of the distant future; we cannot put it out of our minds with the assurance that something will happen before it becomes serious. It is a problem now. It is not a simple problem. Not all lands are crowded. In some cases the problem is more the rate of growth than the absolute population.

The problem of overpopulation is quite different in industrially advanced and in underdeveloped countries. In the latter, rapid increase of agricultural and industrial production is very difficult. Without outside aid a growth rate of two or three percent per year is difficult to sustain over long periods of time. That rate of growth would be encouraging if it meant that living standards rose twenty to thirty percent per decade. But in most such countries the rate of growth of population equals that of production. Immense efforts are needed just to prevent further worsening of the already miserable quality of life. In countries where the population growth rate is very high, the battle is already being lost.

The industrial nations have a quite different problem. If their population growth rates were as large as those of many underdeveloped lands, they, too, would experience difficulties. If the population of the United States doubled in the next twenty years, we would not only have to replace all obsolete facilities, but also double the quantity of homes, factories, highways, schools, hospitals, post offices, food production, and so forth, just to keep up our present standards. This would involve as much production and construction in the next twenty years as we have managed in our total past history; and that would be no mean task even for us! But the population grows much more slowly in this and other industrialized lands. Raising the already comfortable standard of living is not difficult for us.

But it is just in these industrialized lands, and especially in the United States, that the other major problem of overpopulation arises—the problem of overconsumption. It has been estimated that the average American consumes from thirty to fifty times as much of the world's resources as the average Indian. Thus while the increasing population of India creates serious problems for the Indian people, their total impact on the resources of the planet is moderate. We, on the other hand, experience only minor and local ill effects from crowding. But it is our population, and not that of India, that threatens to pollute the skies and oceans and to make the whole world a far poorer place for our descendants.

Those who ridicule the idea that the United States should control its population when there is still much unpeopled land can argue that this country could support ten times its present population. They are right. Ten times our present population could live in this country on the standard of living now endured by the Indian peasant. But if we ask instead whether the world can afford a long continuance of even our present national level of consumption, the answer must be negative. If we wish to continue and pass on to our children anything approaching our present style of life, we are already overpopulated.

Furthermore, the underdeveloped world will not be content to wallow indefinitely in its misery while the industrial nations use up the remainder of the world's irreplaceable resources. A stable world order will require that the industrial nations cooperate with the others in their industrialization also, so that they may have hope of escaping their present treadmill. But it is simply not possible for even the existing world population to consume at the present American rate. There isn't that much to be consumed, and the total resources are declining, not increasing. If we are to set the norm for per capita consumption for the planet, we must learn to consume less as a nation.

I have been speaking of the exhaustible resources of our planet. It is widely recognized that fossil fuels are in limited supply, and it is obvious that if the average per capita consumption of petroleum in the world equaled that in the United States, the world supply would be used up in a few years. The same is true of many metals and minerals.

The story is similar with respect to timber and soil. Even now the forests of the world are being annually reduced. If the rate of consumption of timber products by all people averaged that in the United States, deforestation would be extremely rapid. And if we can conceive of increasing agricultural production around the world to the extent that all people ate as well as we Americans, the already disturbing rate of exhaustion of our topsoils would be accelerated.

Water and electricity are other significant elements in our consumption. Ours is a favored land, but already national rather than merely regional shortages threaten. Water can be reused several times over, but not indefinitely. In most parts of the world, even with the most careful management, the present population could not consume water as we do. There simply is not enough. Similarly, we have nearly exhausted the possibilities of hydroelectric power, and we generate much of our electricity from irreplaceable fossil fuels. There is no possibility of the present population of the world consuming electricity at our rate unless it is generated in other ways.

In making these statements I have largely ignored these other ways, and in them lies some hope. New sources of energy—atomic, for example—will be extensively employed to replace fossil fuels and waterpower. Chemistry will develop plastics to replace metals and minerals, substitutes for wood products will be found, and grains will be grown chemically without use of topsoil.

However, these technological solutions of the

problems caused by the inevitable shortages are themselves extremely dangerous. We have already noted that radioactive wastes continue to pose a danger. In addition, the use of atomic energy generates immense quantities of heat that may seriously alter the temperature of the ocean. The proliferation of chemicals of unknown potency already endangers the living environment, and the rapid increase of dependence on the chemical industry is not compatible with the caution and restraint that are needed.

Furthermore, the replacement of our present dependence on fossil fuels, metals, and topsoil by sophisticated developments in physics and chemistry is an immense undertaking. The required scientific and technological competence is remote from the experience and potentiality of the majority of the world's peoples. The kinds of transformations of cultures that will be required for such changes cannot occur overnight. The world must have time to adjust. It has immense unfinished business dealing with the problems of the pollution it has already created and simply feeding its present population. We dare not accelerate the rate at which technological change will be required for physical survival.

We come finally to the specific warning of the ecologist. It is his province to show us how interrelated are all living things, both plants and animals, that jointly constitute what we call the earth's "biosphere." The destruction of one species of life, however minor it may appear to man, can drastically alter the conditions of life for many other species. Similarly, the introduction of a new species into an area can upset the existing balance. We know too little about the consequences of these kinds of actions to plunge heedlessly on. Yet the rapid rate of change required to meet human demands leaves no time for the careful investigation that we need.

Fifty miles from Los Angeles and a mile above sea level the pines in the San Bernardino Mountains are dying from smog. An attempt is being made to replace them with smog resistant trees. This is a minor incident in the larger picture. But the death of these forests reminds us of the risk of thoughtless tampering with our environment. The survival of life itself may be at stake.

Discussion Questions

1. What problems connected with the ecological crisis seem to you the most important? Why? How are these problems interconnected?
2. What practical solutions to these problems can you envision?
3. Whose fault is the ecological crisis?
4. To what extent might legislation solve the problems?

2

Is Ecology *the* Issue?

The ravages committed by man subvert the relations
and destroy the balance which nature has established;
... and she avenges herself upon the intruder by let-
ting loose upon her defaced provinces her destructive
energies. ... When the forest is gone, the great reser-
voir of moisture stored up in its vegetable mold is
evaporated. ... The well-wooded and humid hills are
turned to ridges of dry rock ... and ... the whole
earth, unless rescued by human art from the physical
degradation to which it tends, becomes an assemblage
of bald mountains, of barren, turfless hills, and of
swampy and malarious plains. There are parts of Asia
Minor, of Northern Africa, of Greece, and even of Al-
pine Europe, where the operation of causes set in action by man has brought the face of the earth to a des-
olation almost as complete as that of the moon. ...
The earth is fast becoming an unfit home for its no-
blest inhabitant, and another era of equal human
crime and human improvidence ... would reduce it to
such a condition of impoverished productiveness, of
shattered surface, of climatic excess, as to threaten the
depravation, barbarism, and perhaps even extinction
of the species.[1]

1. George Perkins Marsh, *Man and Nature,* ed. David
Lowenthal (Cambridge, Mass.: Belknap Press of Harvard
University Press, 1965), pp. 42–43.

These words, which were written over a hundred years ago by George Perkins Marsh, today ring with renewed urgency. America finally heeded the warning of Marsh and saved some of its great forests from irreversible destruction. But new means of destroying the environment, unforeseen by Marsh, threaten now to realize his worst fears. Irven Devore and Richard B. Lee write that "it is still an open question whether man will be able to survive the exceedingly complex and unstable conditions he has created for himself." [2] And David Lyle suggests that "the human race has, maybe, thirty-five years left." [3]

If the threat to survival is as serious as these scientists suggest, then suitable adjustment of our national priorities is the most urgent business of the seventies. The United States cannot solve the world's problems alone, but without American leadership the problems cannot be solved. We are the world's greatest consumers and polluters. We have done more than anyone else to release radiation and new chemicals into our environment. We have the resources to do something about the new problems. Other issues are urgent, but this one is imperative.

The danger in focusing attention on a single issue and raising it as one of supreme importance is that it might seem to detract from the importance of other issues. Those who are struggling for the rights of blacks, or browns, or reds, or students, or women; or for freedom in Brazil, or Greece, or the Soviet Union; or for the survival of Israel or justice for Arab refugees; or for peace in Southeast Asia, feel abandoned and cheated when their erstwhile allies move on to another cause while these battles are far from won.

An allegory will give perspective. Picture the

2. *Esquire,* LXVIII, September 1967, pp. 116–18 ff.
3. *Brookhaven Biology Symposium,* 1969.

world as a ship on a long voyage. The ship has first class and steerage accommodations. The crew directs its attention to the comforts of the first-class passengers, who have plenty of space, luxurious accommodations, and superabundant food of great delicacy and richness. In steerage men and women are crowded and uncomfortable. The food is tasteless and poorly cooked. Some suffer malnutrition. Contagious diseases break out, and medical help is inadequate. Tempers are high, and fights occur. First-class passengers occasionally look down on the steerage deck below with amusement and even with pity, but for the most part they prefer to forget the existence of these other passengers and to enjoy the gracious living for which they have paid. The fact that most of the steerage passengers are of other cultures and races makes this easier.

Many of the steerage passengers dream of someday transferring to first class and a few even succeed in doing so. But most resign themselves to the impossibility of such a move. They live in impotent envy, taking out their anger on each other. Finally, a few among them begin whispering that this is unnecessary. Why should they be crowded and poorly fed when there is so much space and food wasted on other decks? Why not share all the space and food equally?

Many ridicule the idea as impossible, but others listen. Of these, some want to seize by force the space and food they need, while others propose appealing to the innate sense of fair play on the part of the first-class passengers. At first these win out, and a few changes result from their humble and modest requests. The food supply and medical attention are improved. The first-class passengers expect gratitude, but in fact the slight success only intensifies the demands for an equal share.

I will not detail the struggle as it grows bloodier and more bitter. The crew is called in by the first-class passengers to maintain order and guarantee their privileges—for which, after all, they have paid. And the crew obliges with all too little reluctance. The few first-class passengers who sympathize with those in steerage are increasingly ostracized. More important, many of the children of the first-class passengers believe in the cause of the steerage passengers and try to help them. Some of these also fall victim to the crew, while the parents generally think they have gotten what they deserve.

Several times during the struggle the news is heard that the boat has sprung a leak. A few members of the crew are dispatched to see about it. They report that it is not too large a leak yet, although it is growing. Most suppose that the captain will see to it and go on about their business and pleasure. But the captain is too busy trying to keep order, and the few who continue inquiring about the leak are ignored.

The untended leak becomes larger. Some of the ship's supplies are soaked in salt water and ruined. Even the boat's speed is slightly affected. New leaks begin to appear. Although life continues luxurious in first class, some notice that the ship lists a little. Some of the shipboard games are adversely affected. Shuffleboard is abandoned. More voices are raised about the urgency of action, but when the crew shoot some of the children, a new controversy breaks out which distracts attention.

The first-class passengers feel guilty about the killing of these children, but they cannot bring themselves to admit that they are in the wrong. They devote their energies to self-justification. The children are deeply hurt by this attitude on their parents' part. Until now they have felt that the ideals on which they have acted were those of their parents as well and that if only the parents saw the situation clearly they would aid the steerage passengers instead of using force against them. With far less confidence, the steerage passengers have shared this hope. But the willingness of the parents to kill their own children in order to maintain their privileges, and their subsequent justification of this act, is profoundly disillusioning. A few turn to unalloyed violence. Most relapse into angry but lethargic resignation.

The ship continues to list. Almost everyone recognizes it now. But in the aftermath of the intense emotions generated by the other conflicts, no one seems to care very much. Leaders vie with each other to announce their concern, but not one dares to speak realistically of the risk or of the vast cost of dealing with it. The people have no stomach for great sacrifices. Their idealism is spent.

This is where we are now. What happens next is still unsettled. We may continue to fragment into disgruntled minorities while frantic efforts on the part of our leaders to hold us together leave little energy to deal with the spreading leaks. Only when the water covers the lower decks will the passengers turn their attention, too late, to the problems of a sinking ship. With bitter mutual recriminations they will struggle for places in the inadequate lifeboats, while the sinking ship carries most to their death.

Another possibility is that the crew and first class passengers will wall off part of the ship in such a way that although the lower decks fill with water, the steerage passengers drown, and most of the supplies are lost, the ship can stay just barely afloat. In this way many of the first-class passengers can survive, although at a level of subsistence inferior even to that of the steerage passengers when the boat was intact.

A third possibility is that the ship's captain, as a man of wisdom and courage, will persuade all the passengers of the necessity of immediate massive action. Unnecessary supplies are then quickly thrown overboard, including many of the weapons used by the crew to control the steerage passengers. All able-bodied men join together in a massive effort to pump out the water and repair the leaks. In the process, the mutual antagonisms subside. New leadership patterns are established. All the passengers and the crew, as well, become a single community living frugally but harmoniously together.

Granted, only a miracle could realize this third possibility. Politicians would have to refrain from playing upon the mutual antagonisms of our polarized society and challenge us to extremely unpopular sacrifices. Masses of people would have to vote for and follow these politicians. Business and industry would have to adopt new criteria by which to measure achievements, and all of us who are dependent on the present system for our luxuries would have to accept a simpler style of life. Is all that *really* possible?

No one knows; but the unforeseen and the unexpected do occur. Indeed, the rise to consciousness of the ecology/population crisis itself illustrates the openness of the future, the occurrence of the unpredictable, the surprising fruition of forgotten seeds. I myself have been aware of its seriousness only since the summer of 1969. Yet even in that summer and fall one who was concerned felt like a voice crying in the wilderness. No popular national magazine had taken up the issue. The Church seemed silent. Politicians avoided the question. Only a few weary ecologists, nature lovers, and demographers kept up the apparently fruitless struggle to alert the nation before it was too late. The very word ecology was hardly known.

As late as February of 1970, Richard Register could point out the frightening analogy between the human reaction to ecological deterioration and a frog's reaction to the heating of his watery environment:

There is an experiment well known among biologists in which a frog is placed in a large container of water and the temperature is slowly raised. The change is so gradual that the frog shows almost no sign of realizing what's happening. Then, almost peacefully, in temperatures approaching the boiling point, the frog dies—not with a bang, not with a whimper, but in pathetic ignorance.

There is another experiment well known among the inhabitants of Los Angeles in which several million people are placed in a large flat basin bordered by an inversion layer at the desert fringes of that basin. Millions of cars and millions of tons of asphalt and cement are slowly added. The change is so gradual that the population shows almost no sign of realizing what's happening. . . .[4]

But Register's own article was a part of an upsurge of interest. The news media widely took up the new cause. New organizations arose and others gained fresh momentum and vitality. Politicians vied with each other in showing their concern. Ecologists and naturalists were in great demand. Ecology became a household word, and cars sprouted bumper stickers urging people to "control your local stork."

But there are already signs of waning interest! One hears flippant talk of someone having taken his eco-trip and being ready for something else. The events in Cambodia and at Kent State displaced ecological concerns on the college campuses.

At a superficial level this is inevitable. As soon as we move from description of the problem to proposals for action, we lose much of our confidence and conviction. No one really knows enough to answer our questions. Economists and ecologists often speak at cross-purposes, and we must listen to both. The issue is tied up with every other issue, and any step we take toward its solution has ramifications in other areas

4. *Los Angeles Times.*

that are often bitter indeed. Many leftists are resentful about the emergence of this concern, since it distracts attention from their call for a social revolution. Rightists regard it all as a Communist plot, since the problems cannot be solved without radical changes in our way of life.

It is profoundly unfortunate for our national health that our attention span is so limited. The problems of crime, race, and violence do not disappear when we turn to something else. Similarly, our environment will not recover from our assault upon it when we stop thinking about it.

For a while at least, our new attention to the environment will probably generate new interests. Now that we notice such matters, we find ever new indications of the seriousness of the situation. The recent discovery of mercury in our rivers is a case in point. The disappearance of various species of wildlife will not now go unheralded. We will be observant of our weather to see how it is being affected by our actions. The attention of the world focuses on the army as it dumps nerve gases into the ocean. If supersonic transports are as destructive as many expect, that destruction will not go unnoticed. There will be more public clamor against the commercialization of our remaining wilderness. Industry will have to consider more carefully how it disposes of its wastes.

But the question remains whether all this will lead only to a series of *ad hoc* measures designed to meet particular emergencies when public opinion demands it, or whether it will lead to careful planning and rethinking of our national life. The latter can occur only if a *new vision* of man and his place in relation to nature comes into being, a vision that would naturally express itself in a changed style of life.

Discussion Questions

1. Is human survival really at stake, or are the alarmed scientists exaggerating the issue? Discuss.
2. What is the responsibility and potentiality of the United States in confronting ecological problems? Why?
3. Discuss the allegory of the leaking ship and the options presented for survival. Is the comparison convincing?
4. Can a change in attitude lead to a change in behavior? What change of attitude is needed if ecological problems are to be solved?

3

Let the Engineers Handle It!

To a very large extent the problems now confronting us are technological. We must find means of disposing of our wastes that do not continue to poison land, sea, and air. We must find ways of generating energy that are less ecologically destructive. We must develop new modes of transportation. We must learn how to reuse much that we now throw away in ever mounting garbage heaps. We must develop new strains of rice and wheat to further the "green revolution" in the tropical world. New and simplified techniques of birth control must be found. These are all technological problems.

There is always the danger that this discussion of the philosophical and theological vision that is needed to deal with the ecological problems might seem to imply some disparagement of these technological tasks. It does not. But it does imply that the problems we face are not *merely* technological. We cannot simply continue to live and think as we have while assigning to the engineers the task of restoring the earth.

An important illustration of the problem is the now oft-told story of the Aswan Dam in Egypt. Few countries suffer more acutely from the worldwide problem of overpopulation than does Egypt. For years it has depended on importing wheat for its survival. The modern, aggressive government under Nasser determined to deal with this situation. To produce more food required that more land be brought under cultivation. In Egypt this could be done only by irrigation. By constructing a dam not only could water be made available for irrigation, but also immense quantities of electrical energy could be generated to facilitate the industrialization of the nation. Forward-looking Egyptians carried through the project against all kinds of obstacles including the American government's withdrawal of support.

However, *Time* magazine reports:

When an international team of ecologists studied the effects of the dam, they were shocked. For one thing, waterweeds are clogging the shoreline of Lake Nasser behind the dam. The weeds may well speed evaporation through transpiration to the point where the lake lacks enough water to drive the gigantic generators.

The dam has also stopped the flow of silt down the Nile, which in the past offset the natural erosion of the land from the Nile delta. As a result, downstream erosion may wash away as much productive farm land as is opened up by new irrigation systems around Lake Nasser. Without the nutrient-rich silt reaching the Mediterranean, the Egyptian sardine catch declined from 18,000 tons in 1965 to 500 tons in 1968. As a final penalty, irrigation projects on the delta plain have allowed a moisture-loving snail to thrive. Since it carries schistosomiasis, most of the delta people have had that agonizing liver and intestinal disease.[1]

This story does not indict technology as such, and even in the instance cited, arguments may be given for the course of action followed. But it does indicate cer-

1. "Fighting to Save the Earth from Man," 2 February 1970.

tain limitations of the technological attitude. We need to become clearer about these limitations.

In the first place, the function of technology is to manipulate, whereas what the subhuman world often needs is to be left alone. Here it is the whole tenor of our culture that is called into question. Raw or untamed nature cries aloud in our tradition for man to enter it to rule, to exploit, and to impose his own patterns of order. A beautiful wilderness area calls for "development." Wild animals are to be hunted, tamed, or put into zoos. An inaccessible area calls for roads and bridges. A meadow calls for cattle to graze it. A virgin forest calls for a sawmill and logging roads. When we do preserve some bits of our land from strictly economic exploitation, it is as scenery, as campsites, and for nature study. For these too, a certain amount of "development" is required.

Much of our manipulation of nature is highly desirable and even necessary. Without it, no properly human life would be possible. Also, where man has seriously wounded the subhuman world he cannot simply stand back and leave it to itself. Many species of wildlife would have died out altogether if they were not preserved in parks and zoos. The disappearance of forests would be accelerated if man did not fight forest fires. But this interventionist solution, to which we resort so readily, is sometimes more destructive than helpful in the long run. Often what the subhuman world needs most is for man to leave it to itself. Given time and space it has immense powers of rejuvenation. But unless we can hold in check our technological mentality, unless we can guide our actions by a new consciousness or vision, we will not allow the subhuman world the time and space it needs.

The vision we need involves the conviction that the worth of the subhuman world is not only its usefulness to us but also its value in itself. With this vision man can develop the willingness to share his planet with other creatures. Then we will leave places here and there where the evolutionary processes that have produced these wonders, including ourselves, can continue unchecked. To these ends technology is irrelevant, and the technological attitude that has shaped us all is antithetical.

Technology and the technological attitude have a second limitation which is determined by their masters. They have developed chiefly in the service of economics and military power. Both of these have operated on the assumption that the subhuman world has value only as it furthers pragmatic human ends. They have seen man's environment as an essentially inexhaustible source of supplies to be possessed and processed. The whole engineering tradition is geared to the production of as much wealth or destructive power as possible, without regard to the question of long-range exhaustion of resources or pollution of the environment. This tradition will be transformed only if the total climate of opinion is transformed, and if society is reorganized to make its decisions in terms of long-range considerations of survival and well-being.

Thus far, hardly a beginning has been made toward such a change. Economic considerations remain dominant, and technology continues to serve these even where our very limited knowledge of the ecological need is quite sufficient to dictate changes. The government's vigorous support of the SST program is the most glaring current instance. The only justification for building the SST is that otherwise the United States will lose out to Britain, France, and the Soviet Union in the competition to supply planes to the world's airlines. According to our technological consciousness, bigger and faster airplanes constitute progress regardless of consequences and despite the fact that they are not needed. Since this technological consciousness will produce an economic demand for them, the administration affirmed that they should be produced, even though we already know they will be immensely destructive.

Fortunately, Congress refused to continue subsidizing this dangerous monster. It seems obvious that the sensible response to the threat of other nations' building and marketing SSTs would be to make clear that we will never allow them to fly over our country or to land at our airports. Since much of the projected use of these planes involves our airports, such a step alone would greatly discourage further development of the SST. In addition, some nations have already taken this step, and others would follow suit —especially if we led the way. We should seek through the United Nations to weld world opinion against these planes. Our national policy, if geared to saving the habitability of the planet instead of economic competition, would give priority to such matters.

This points to a third limitation of technology and the technological attitude. It embodies a false understanding of the relation of ends and means.

John Dewey used to stress that ends and means cannot be separated. Every end is a means to some further end. He was correct. But it is equally important to stress that every living thing is not only a means to be made use of by others but also an end in itself.

The technological attitude, however, makes a sharp distinction between ends and means. The engineer is to have ends assigned him. His task is to discover and execute the most efficient means of achieving those ends. This leads to systematic blindness in three directions.

First, however sensitive he may be incidentally as

a human being, the engineer as engineer does not regard the intrinsic value of the existing state of affairs
with which his enterprise must interfere. He views the
environment that he will alter as instrument or obstacle to his assigned purposes. Everything not specified
for him as ends to be achieved is reduced to purely instrumental status.

Second, he does not attend to the incidental effects of tampering with the existing state of affairs.
When he builds a dam he does not consider the long-
term effects of changes in the aquatic life, even when
these may affect the interests of fishermen and hunt-
ers. His attention is concentrated on achieving the assigned goal.

Third, it is not for the technologist to consider
the wider implications and long-term consequences of
achieving the goal. If the SST he is building proves in
the end not even economically beneficial, that is of no
concern to him. If it leaves vapor trails in the strato-
sphere, that is for other engineers to worry about
later. His task involves consideration of such matters
only if relevant specifications are included from the
first as part of his assigned end.

There would be nothing wrong with this if the
technological attitude belonged only to the engineer.
Somewhere there must be this concentration of attention on the efficient attainment of goals. But the technological attitude also affects those who set the goals.
They aim at the winning of a war, or improvement in
the balance of payments, or bringing more land under
cultivation, or increasing the output of automobiles,
with just the same isolation of ends from means that
characterizes the engineer. Business and military life
are compartmentalized. One is trained to consider particular aspects of the total situation as alone relevant
and to appraise means for achieving desired ends simply in terms of those ends. Other consequences, either

of the means employed or of the end achieved, are neglected.

What does one do today if he suffers from dizzy
spells and does not know whether they are psychological or physical in origin? Perhaps you will say that he
should first check the possibility of organic causes.
Well and good. But he cannot simply go to "a doctor."
There are doctors for skin, for feet, for hearts, for sinuses, for bones, for the sexual organs, and so forth. To
what doctor then? If he knew what was causing the
dizziness, the answer would be simple. But we are assuming he doesn't know. Who can tell him?

Perhaps we can advise him a little further. Dizziness might mean there was something wrong with the
digestive tract, or with the ear, or with the circulatory
system, or with the eyes. Of course there are other possibilities. Maybe he is simply overworked and would
be cured by a rest. But how is he to find out? Must he
diagnose himself before he can decide which doctor to
go to? Or can he perhaps still find a general practi-
tioner or skilled diagnostician who can help him?

Many doctors know that all the parts of the body
interact with each other and with a man's emotions as
well. They know that this complex interaction of the
parts with each other and with the whole is neglected
when they treat only bits and pieces of the organism.
Yet the pressures for specialization are immense, and
with it comes, inevitably, the technological attitude.

Just as there are some doctors who resist the technological attitude and the accompanying specialization, so there are also some scientists who resist it. Of
these, the most important for our present purposes are
the ecologists. The ecologist insists that just as we do
not have a multiplicity of parts of a body which are
then only incidentally related to each other as a
human being, so we do not have in the living world
about us a multiplicity of individual entities which

then have certain incidental relations with each other. When we study them in isolation from each other we do not understand them. The individual organism is constituted by its relations with other entities. Its dependence on these is not secondary but primary. Every change in one part of the ecological system affects the whole system.

The ecological attitude is the reverse of the technological one. It does not view the individual action in terms only of the end toward which it is directed but in terms of the whole network of effects that will actually follow from it. Each of these effects is in turn viewed as important both in itself and for the further effects that will follow from it. The ecological attitude does not put an end to manipulation of the environment, but whereas the technological attitude breeds confidence and ruthless haste, the ecological attitude breeds hesitation and caution. Whereas the technological attitude directs energies toward short-term goals, assured that new problems can be dealt with as they arise, the ecological attitude attends to complex and poorly understood consequences that may take years to work themselves out. The technological attitude assumes that with time all things are possible. It projects a future society of unlimited comfort, convenience, pleasure, and luxury, and unlimited extension through space and time. The ecological attitude suggests that the price of technological and economic progress may be too high, that there are limits, perhaps rather narrow ones, beyond which man cannot go, and that we must adjust to them soon or perish.

Discussion Questions

1. In what ways are the problems facing us merely technological? Why?

2. Does the subhuman world have a value in itself? Explain.
3. Can we have technology without the technological attitude?
4. How does the ecological attitude differ from the technological? Are both attitudes valuable and important? Which is the more important?

4

The Christian Responsibility

Until recently, agriculture has been the chief occupa-
tion even in "advanced" societies, hence, any change
in methods of tillage has much importance. Early
plows, drawn by two oxen, did not normally turn the
sod but merely scratched it. Thus, cross-plowing was
needed and fields tended to be squarish. In the fairly
light soils and semi-arid climates of the Near East and
Mediterranean this worked well. But such a plow was
inappropriate to the wet climate and often sticky soils
of northern Europe. By the latter part of the seventh
century after Christ, however, following obscure begin-
nings, certain northern peasants were using an entirely
new kind of plow, equipped with a vertical knife to
cut the line of the furrow, a horizontal share to
slice under the sod, and a moldboard to turn it over. The
friction of this plow with the soil was so great that it
normally required not two but eight oxen. It attacked
the land with such violence that cross-plowing was not
needed, and fields tended to be shaped in long strips.

In the days of the scratch-plow, fields were distrib-
uted generally in units capable of supporting a single
family. Subsistence farming was the presupposition.
But no peasant owned eight oxen; to use the new and
more efficient plow, peasants pooled their oxen to
form plow-teams, originally receiving (it would appear) plowed strips in proportion to their contribution. Thus, distribution of land was based no longer
on the needs of a family but, rather, on the capacity

of a power machine to till the earth. Man's relation to the soil was profoundly changed. Formerly man had been part of nature; now he was the exploiter of nature. Nowhere else in the world did farmers develop any analogous agricultural implement. Is it coincidence that modern technology, with its ruthlessness toward nature, has so largely been produced by descendants of these peasants of northern Europe? [1]

The author of these words, Lynn White, Jr., shows that technological developments in Western Europe did not await the rise of Western science or of a generally high level of culture. On the contrary, there were surprising advances even in the period sometimes known as the Dark Ages. By the year 1000 Western Europeans were applying water power not only to milling grain but to other industrial processes as well. By the early fourteenth century they had developed in two forms the weight-driven mechanical clock. When the Greek ecclesiastic, Bessarion, visited Italy in the mid-fifteenth century, he was amazed by the superiority of Western ships, arms, textiles, and glass, and especially by the waterwheels that sawed timber and pumped the bellows of blast furnaces. Later in the century it was technological supremacy that enabled even small Western European nations like Portugal to explore, conquer, and settle large parts of the globe.

These facts indicate the great importance of technological developments in shaping human society and human history. But in "The Historical Roots of Our Ecological Crisis" White is asking a different question. Why did these events occur in Western Europe when it was not the center of civilization? Obviously they

1. Lynn White, Jr., "The Historical Roots of Our Ecological Crisis," *Science* CLV (March 10, 1967), pp. 1203–07; in Garrett De Bell, ed., *The Environmental Handbook* (New York: Ballantine Books, 1970).

cannot be attributed to superior intelligence or native genius. The question to be asked is why these peasants and artisans, even when the level of their general culture was primitive, turned their energies to technological developments in an unparalleled way.

The answer to this question can be found in their peculiar attitude, especially their view of the relation of man and nature. This attitude was expressed in visual form in the early Middle Ages in pictures of man receiving nature from God as his fiefdom. White notes that Frankish calendars "show men coercing the world around them—plowing, harvesting, chopping trees, and butchering pigs. Man and nature are two things, and man is master." [2]

The question as to the attitude that was conducive to the rise of technology is not raised simply out of curiosity about the past. That attitude is still present. The first Genesis account of creation, with its specific authorization of man's dominance over the rest of the world, continued to be effectively operative in the West through the eighteenth century. Even when biblical authority became questionable in the nineteenth century, the vision of man's lordship over the subhuman world was not doubted. On the contrary, man's rightful domination was supposed to be self-evident and not dependent on the authority of revelation. Even the rise of evolutionary theory did little to give man a sense of kinship with other animals. Western man's unwillingness to leave things alone, to let the subhuman world be, stems directly from this deep-seated Western common sense.

White's paper was addressed to a national assembly of scientists. His major thesis was that as long as the attitude and vision that have given rise to the ecological crisis continue unchanged, the problem is insol-

2. *Ibid.*

uble. Furthermore, the technology that has developed within the context of this attitude cannot be the instrument of its change. Since the attitude that is responsible for our difficulties is a religious or theological one, the change that is required must be at that level. Thus, White challenged the assumptions of those scientists who see all of man's real problems as falling within the sphere of science and technology. He also challenged the complacency of Christians. Christianity is, at least in part, responsible for the technological attitude that has brought about our crisis and that still impedes effective action. Christian theologians must share in the rethinking of basic attitudes about man and his environment.

White shows the surprising extent of the independence of the development of technology from scientific advances. Even the industrial revolution occurred with little influence from any advanced science. The two were first effectively related in the chemical industries of the eighteenth century. The general application of scientific knowledge to technology began only in the middle of the nineteenth century.

Although technology alone has enabled man to change the face of nature, the present global crisis has emerged from the modern wedding of science and technology. Hence science shares with technology in responsibility for the threatening ecological disaster.

Earlier generations stressed the tension between science and Christian theology. Often their purpose was to discredit Christianity. They thought of science as a product of a reason free from religious faith or they attributed it to the Greek influence in the Renaissance. But more careful consideration from a less prejudiced point of view shows that the development of science in the West began in the high Middle Ages. It was continuous with the rest of the cultural activity and conviction of the time, and this was profoundly shaped by Christianity. The minds of the scientists were certainly free; but so were those of the philosophers and theologians of the period. A free mind is not one that is unaffected by its history or by the climate of opinion of its time.

Science can flourish when men believe that behind the apparent randomness or willfulness of phenomena there is an enduring order to be discovered. The understanding of reality as cosmos enabled the Greeks to make a brilliant start in the development of science, but on the whole, they preferred rational deductions to painstaking investigation of the facts. Islam made contributions—especially in medicine.

But it was the Western Christian view of nature as the creation of an intelligent will that provided the context and motivation for the sustained and patient effort, divorced from all consideration of practical results, that carried Western European science from its infancy in the Middle Ages to the amazing achievements of the seventeenth century. Because nature was seen as God's creation, one knew that it embodied rational and intelligible order. Furthermore, the discovery of *that* order was of supreme value since it led to knowledge of God himself.

Aspects of Christian belief have thus been responsible for Western European advances in both technology and science. Whereas that might have sounded like boasting a short time ago, in the light of our present problems it has the ring of confession. In this connection, there is still another basic aspect of Christian belief that has played its role in bringing history to its present pass. The Judeo-Christian tradition has deeply implanted in the Western psyche the idea that every human individual is of absolute value. Of course, the actions of nations and individuals have repeatedly violated this principle. But that is not the point. The positive effect of the principle on national and individual action has been enormous. Vast efforts have been expended to keep alive human beings whether or not they are able to make a contribution to society. A large portion of scientific and technological advancement has been successfully directed toward the conquest of disease and the prolongation of life. The Westernization of the globe in this respect has played a major role in the vast increase in worldwide population in the last fifty years.

When this high appraisal of the value of the human individual is brought together, as it has been in Western Christianity, with the view that man is called to dominate the subhuman world, this world is still further reduced in value. Indeed, it has been denied any value in itself. Its value lies entirely in its usefulness to man. Only man has intrinsic worth. The value of the subhuman world is purely instrumental.

These convictions have provided the overarching context for our technological dealing with the world. If they remain intact and continue to govern our use of technology, what consequences can we expect to follow? We might continue basically on the course we have followed thus far. We would then view the progressive breakdown of the ecological cycle as reason for accelerating our scientific investigations and technological progress. We have already moved far toward substituting an artificial environment for a natural one. If the planet cannot support both a vastly increased human population and high grades of subhuman life, we would destroy the latter and learn to produce what we need artificially out of the inanimate resources of the planet or from the lowest grades of the animate. We would build vast cities under plastic domes surrounded by poisoned air, polluted water, rock, and dust. The subhuman world would then indeed be little more than the mere "it" we have treated it as being.

Whether such a direction is even possible no one today really knows. Could science and technology sustain a larger population in this wholly artificial context than can be sustained by achieving ecological balance? Would it turn out that man has either biological or psychological needs that could not be met in this way? Would the changes in temperature, sea level, and radiation be so drastic that survival would be impossible despite scientific progress?

Even if this direction were possible, one may question the wisdom of those who would choose it. The attempt to evaluate a type of life profoundly different from any we have known is fraught with hazards. It is difficult to think of existence in such a world as even human, much less happy. The absolutization of human life at the total expense of subhuman life seems to lead to a mode of being in which human existence itself would be subhuman in quality.

In any case, we know that we do not presently have the science or technology to sustain human life on a dead planet. If we press on in this direction, most of the world's present population and its immediate offspring must be sacrificed. Perhaps a hundred or a thousand years from now men will be faced with a serious choice between increasing population and retaining a living environment, but today the living context remains essential to the maintenance of human life as well.

On this ground alone, then, one who holds the traditional evaluation of man and nature should agree to devote vast energies to nursing the environment back to health while stabilizing population. At present, subhuman life is necessary to man's existence and, therefore, of immeasurable instrumental value.

Without a recognition that man *needs* a healthy environment, there is no possibility of making the changes required to heal the subhuman world. Self-interest is a necessary motivation, but it is not sufficient. This insufficiency was illustrated in the conservation movement. As a leader in that movement, Aldo Leopold noted its actual impact. In the thirties farmers were called on to adopt new approaches in the name of enlightened self-interest. They responded well. But in the absence of disinterested concern for their land, they adopted only those practices such as contour farming that had short-run economic advantages. In *A Sand County Almanac* Leopold wrote in 1949 that "the education actually in progress makes no mention of obligations to land over and above those dictated by self-interest. The net result is that we have more education but less soil, fewer healthy woods, and as many floods as in 1937." [3]

Discussion Questions

1. What do you think is the genuinely Christian attitude to man's role in the world? To technology? To the value of the subhuman world?
2. How did the Western Christian view of nature contribute to the advance of science?
3. Does the "absolute" value of man mean that nothing else has any value? That other things have only instrumental value? That human beings should be multiplied without restraint? That man has no responsibility? Do you think man has any absolute value?
4. Can we change our behavior toward the environment without changing our attitude?

3. (New York: Oxford University Press, Inc., 1949); (New York: Ballantine Books, Inc., 1970), p. 245.

5

Non-Western Views of Nature

In *The Making of a Counter Culture* Theodore
Roszak gives voice to the horror with which many
sensitive persons view our dominant inherited attitude toward nature. "Whatever our degree of intellectual sophistication," he writes, "we shall as a culture
continue to deal with our natural environment as lov-
ingly, as reverently as a butcher deals with the carcass
of a dead beast." [1] To throw into relief the harsh bru-
tality of our dominant practice, he quotes a Wintu Indian woman describing the contrasting relation of her
shamanistic culture and that of the white man to a
common environment.

The white people never cared for the land or deer or
bear. When we Indians kill meat, we eat it all up.
When we dig roots, we make little holes. . . . We shake
down acorns and pinenuts. We don't chop down trees.
We only use dead wood. But the white people plow
up the ground, pull up the trees, kill everything. The
tree says, "Don't. I am sore. Don't hurt me." But they
chop it down and chop it up. The spirit of the land
hates them. . . . The Indians never hurt anything, but
the white people destroy all. They blast rocks and scat-
ter them on the ground. The rock says, "Don't! You
are hurting me." But the white people pay no atten-

1. (Garden City, N.Y.: Doubleday & Co., 1969), p. 258.

tion. When the Indians use rocks, they take little round ones for their cooking.... How can the spirit of the earth like the white man?... Everywhere the white man has touched it, it is sore.[2]

We can immediately sense the ecological significance of such a passage. Here is a people who seek in every possible way not to interfere with their environment. Their motivation is not the man-centered one we have been considering. Instead, it includes a concern for trees and rocks that is like that for other human beings. Self-interest plays a role, since the Indians desire that the spirit of the earth like them. But pragmatic estimates of consequences to themselves are not primary. The Indians have observed the white man getting away with it for generations. What is primary for them is a vision of reality in which they and their world belong together in a unity.

Stewart Udall in *The Quiet Crisis* writes:

The most common trait of all primitive peoples is a reverence for the live-giving earth, and the native American shared this elemental ethic: the land was alive to his loving touch, and he, its son, was brother to all creatures. His feelings were made visible in medicine bundles and dance rhythms for rain, and all of his religious rites and land attitudes savored the inseparable world of nature and God, the Master of Life. During the long Indian tenure the land remained undefiled save for scars no deeper than the scratches of cornfield clearings or the farming canals of the Hobokams on the Arizona desert.[3]

Primitive men hunt animals for food. But they sense in the destruction of animal life a violation of

2. *Ibid.,* p. 245.
3. (New York: Holt, Rinehart & Winston, 1964), p. 4; (New York: Avon Books, 1970).

the animal that must somehow be atoned. They often ask the pardon of their animal victims when it is their painful duty to kill. The primitive Kafirs hunted the elephant. But when they had killed it, they assured it they had not done so on purpose.

If men had remained primitive in spirit our ecological crisis would not have arisen. Primitive life was in fundamental balance and harmony with the animate and inanimate world around it. This harmony was not mere chance or simply the result of the lack of means for mastering and destroying the environment. Mastery and destruction were not sought. The aim was rather to leave the environment alone as much as possible, to interfere with it only as necessary for the well-being of the tribe, and to surround these interferences with ceremonies designed to express their exceptional and unfortunate character.

The difference between primitive man and ourselves is not to be interpreted as a relative lack of intelligence. His language is very complex and expresses many distinctions we do not ordinarily perceive. He has an awareness of distinctive features of the world which escape our attention. But as Ernst Cassirer notes in *An Essay on Man,*

... in his conception of nature and life all these differences are obliterated by a stronger feeling: the deep conviction of a fundamental and indelible solidarity of life that bridges over the multiplicity and variety of its single forms. He does not ascribe to himself a unique and privileged place in the scale of nature. The consanguinity of all forms of life seems to be a general presupposition of mythical thought.[4]

Thus the difference between primitive man and ourselves is a difference in mode of consciousness. We

4. (Garden City, N.Y.: Doubleday & Co., Anchor Book, 1953), p. 109.

experience our worlds differently. Whereas we objec-
tify our world, he participates in his. We seek and at-
tain dominance. He seeks and attains balance.

Does this mean that the new consciousness that
we need is the consciousness already realized in the
primitive? Roszak does not go quite that far. He
knows that there can be no simple return to the past.
Yet he does see in the primitive shaman a model for
the consciousness we need. Is he right?

At one level he seems to be. We would be en-
riched if we could recover the immediacy and intimacy of the primitive's relation to plants and animals.
The primitive's respect for the world and his effort to
live in harmony with it could guide our responses to
the ecological crisis. This spirit of kinship and unity
would check our spirit of conquest and indifference.

But Roszak goes much too far in idealizing the
primitive vision. Although there was warmth and joy
in the primitive's intimacy with nature, there was also
terror and guilt. As Erich Neumann aptly describes it:

Exposed to the dark forces of the world and the unconscious, early man's feeling is necessarily one of con-
stant endangerment. Life in the psychic cosmos of the
primitive is a life full of danger and uncertainty; and
the daemonism of the external world, with its sickness
and death, famines and floods, droughts and earthquakes, is heightened beyond measure when contami-
nated with what we call the inner world.[5]

We must realize also that the failure to distinguish sharply between men and subhuman entities not
only caused primitive man to respect the latter more
but also to respect the former less. Human life was
comparatively cheap. In overcoming our alienation

5. *The Origins and History of Consciousness*, 2 vols.
(New York: Harper & Brothers Torchbook, 1954), p. 40.

from nature, a return to the primitive consciousness would involve also the loss of our hard won sense of human dignity and worth.

Further, the vision of the primitive did not prevent him from adopting ecologically destructive practices. On occasion the Indian drove herds of buffalo over cliffs and then ate only their tongues. With the advent of the horse, he increased his rate of killing the buffalo so much that some scholars believe he would have exterminated the herds even without the aid of the white man.

Finally, there are practical considerations. If we were so foolish as to attempt a return to a primitive world the vast majority of us would have to die. The present population is supported by aggressively modifying and utilizing the environment in a way alien to the primitive spirit. With the bear and the buffalo, and the wild turkey and the beaver almost gone, and the fish in many rivers killed by pollution, the American land could not support even the pre-Columbian Indian population if we lived as they did—and that was a tiny population in comparison with ours.

Of course there is no possibility of return to the past, however idyllic it may appear, but if we could and did return, we would be appalled by the actuality of what we found. As a result, if the choice were between moving forward toward a wholly artificial environment, with technology almost wholly replacing the natural environment, and returning to a primitive existence, we would be forced to choose the former, however horrible it might be.

However, the choice may not need to be between a primitive existence and a fully technologized one. In the Orient, high civilizations have been built in conjunction with sophisticated views of reality that nevertheless share with the primitive the sense of balance and harmony with nature.

In Israel man established himself as man by distinguishing himself from the rest of nature and setting himself apart from it. To some extent this was true also of Confucianism in China. But the deeper Chinese vision did not accept this divorce of man from nature. In Western painting the subhuman world sometimes appears as background or context for human presence or action, sometimes as artifact, or as game, or as still life, and occasionally as somewhat anthropomorphized or sentimentalized wilderness from which man is absent. Man can hardly appear in Western art without dominating the scene. In Chinese landscape painting, on the other hand, man is presented as part of nature, harmoniously related to the whole, but no more than one part among others.

The influential concept of *fêng-shui* involves the adaptation of human buildings and roads to the cosmic spirit or breath. This leads to construction that blends into the landscape rather than dominating it. Natural curves are preferred to straight lines.

This Chinese vision is in greater continuity with the primitive vision than is the humanism of Israel or Confucius; but it is far from primitive. Especially in its Taoist form, it represents a position of high sophistication and great appeal to the cultivated Western mind. In Taoism the goal is the recovery or renewal of the primordial harmony of heaven and earth. This is not achieved by intervention in the world, either human or subhuman, but by *in*action. As George Foot Moore notes: "Not to bring the universe, by activities of any kind, into harmony with man's desires, but by pure passivity to be in harmony with the universe, is the way to be blessed." [6]

To prize inaction does not mean literally to give

6. *History of Religions*, vol. 1 (New York: Charles Scribner's Sons, 1946), p. 55.

up all physical movement. What it does mean is to give up interference in the course of society or nature. Well-intentioned social reforms are just as objectionable in this respect as are sinister manipulations for selfish ends. Men should avoid intervention in the natural simplicities rather than try to shape events to fit their purposes.

The ideal quality of life expresses itself in gentleness, humility, and frugality. But these are not virtues to be strenuously cultivated. Rather they are the consequences that follow the abandonment of all desire that things be other than they are. Contentment with life as it is allows the individual's existence to blend with encompassing *Tao*—that is, the original and fundamental and unchanging Way.

The Great Tao is all pervasive; it may be seen on the right and on the left.

All things depend on it, and are produced; it denies itself to none.

It achieves its works of merit, but has no name or reputation. With tenderness it nourishes all things, yet claims no lordship over them.

It is ever passionless, and may be named among the smallest things.

All things submit to it, yet it claims no lordship over them, it may be called great.

Thus the Sage to the end of his life never exalts himself; and thus he is able to achieve great things.[7]

If the Taoist attitude had dominated human history, technology and science would not have developed. Men would not have been driven to preserve and extend human life. The natural cycles of abun-

7. "Tao Teh King, #34," in S. E. Frost, ed., *The Sacred Writings of the World's Great Religions* (New York: The New Home Library, 1943). Available as *Tao Te Ching*, trans. D. C. Lau (Baltimore, Md.: Penguin Books, 1963).

dance and famine would have continued to be accompanied by the increase and decrease of population. Men would have accepted these cyclical changes without resentment or ambition. There would be no ecological crisis.

At first glance Taoism seems to have the advantages of the primitive consciousness without its liabilities. The Taoist has no terror of either the external or the internal world. He is also free from guilt. He is not, like the primitive, undiscriminating in his reactions or lacking in freedom. He knows human life as human and values it as such. Moreover, the Taoist vision seems to have been compatible with the long survival of a great nation with advanced technology.

Nevertheless, before we suppose that in Taoism we have the consciousness that is needed, we should note the historical facts. Taoism did not control actual Chinese practice in relation to the natural environment. The Chinese deforested vast areas of their land as thoroughly as did any other people despite some awareness of the consequences. When the aesthetic and passive preferences of the Chinese conflicted with their economic needs, the latter were generally determinative. Although some Taoists refused to employ technological advances, Chinese society as a whole prized them. The Taoist passivity in relation to social and political processes restrained Taoists from preventing the ecologically destructive practices of others.

If Chinese deforestation and other ecologically destructive practices were simply typical of all populous civilizations, it would count but little as an objection to our adoption of Taoism today. But we find that in much of Western Europe there has been a sustained and quite successful effort to save large sections of forests. It is *Communist* China, which shares the Western passion for mastery and use, that is engaged in widespread efforts at reforestation. In this respect the attitude of dominating nature has worked better than the more quiescent Taoist one. Domination can mean careful and sustained management rather than ruthless destruction. Even if destruction represents lack of foresight and planning rather than the desire to master and control, it is still destruction, and all the disastrous consequences follow. If we adopted the Taoist attitude today, the results would more likely be continued deterioration of our resources rather than effective conservation.

Here, too, Marsh's vision was prophetic. Man cannot now leave a wounded nature to her fate. Instead, he must

... become a co-worker with nature in the reconstruction of the damaged fabric which the negligence and wantonness of former lodgers has rendered untenable. He must aid her in reclothing the mountain slopes with forests and vegetable mould, thereby restoring the fountains which she provided to water them; in checking the devastating fury of torrents, and bringing back the surface drainage to its primitive narrow channels.[8]

What we need, then, are active efforts to save our environment based on adequate scientific information and technological skill. The vision we require is one that would encourage and guide long-range planning and vigorous efforts. To this end, neither the primitive nor the Taoist vision would be effective.

Discussion Questions

1. What is the primitive's attitude toward man and the subhuman world? Is the primitive's

8. *Op. cit.*, pp. 35–36.

sense of participation in nature better than Western man's sense of separation?

2. What is the Taoist attitude toward human interference in the course of society and nature? Does it remind you of any Western economic systems? Is Taoism desirable or practical in today's world?

6

A New Christianity

If the continuation of our present direction leads to horror, if the return to a primitive consciousness is impossible, and if we cannot afford the quiescence and poise of Taoism when so many changes are needed, where shall we turn? The answer is that rather than seek to recover something that is lost or to leap into an alien tradition we need to go forward in the transformation of the tradition in which we now stand. To do so, we should seek within our tradition those submerged elements whose new prominence would give us the vision or consciousness we need.

In Christian history there are two figures who stand out for their participation in the consciousness we need: Francis of Assisi and Albert Schweitzer. Francis' respect for his brother the wolf and his sisters the birds was not less real than that of the primitive, but it differed profoundly. He did not abandon Western rationality; he went beyond it. He knew none of the guilt that pervades the lives of primitives. Although his life was hardly less precarious than theirs, he did not share their terror.

Francis may be too remote from our skeptical day to be a persuasive teacher. Probably his practice was too extreme to serve as an effective model of the new Christianity. Few of us will want to preach to birds. But this objection does not apply to Schweitzer. He lived among us very much as a citizen of our time. In turning his back upon the comforts and advantages of a successful life in Europe he was not rejecting the achievements of European culture. He continued throughout his life to contribute to the philosophy and theology of Europe as well as to its music. It was *modern* medicine he went to Africa to practice. Further, Schweitzer was free from sentimentality. He was not credulous. Few Western humanists find his ideas difficult to understand.

What Western humanists and Christians do find difficult is to adopt Schweitzer's self-giving devotion to the service of human need and his vision of all life as worthy of reverence. The former stands squarely in the tradition of Christian devotion. The latter transcends or extends it.

In Schweitzer's words:

The ethics of reverence for life is the ethics of Jesus, philosophically expressed, made cosmic in scope, and conceived as intellectually necessary.

The great error of earlier ethics is that it concerned itself only with the relations of man to man. The real question is, however, one concerning man's relations to the world and to all life which comes within his reach. A man is ethical only when life, as such, is holy to him, that is, the lives of plants and animals as well as the lives of men. Moreover, he is ethical also only when he extends help to all life that is in need of it. Only the universal ethics of the ever-expanding sense of responsibility for all life can be grounded in thought. The ethics of the relation of man to man is not something unto itself. It is only a particular application of universal ethics.[1]

1. *Out of My Life and Thought,* ed. C. T. Campion (New York: Holt, Rinehart & Winston, 1949; New York: New American Library, Mentor Books, 1953, p. 126.)

Thus it is clear that the extension of concern to all living things is neither a movement backward nor away from our Christian heritage. It is a movement forward in the inner transformation and further development of this peculiar tradition.

The tradition began in ancient Israel. Israel grew out of the primitive immersion in nature by affirming man's primacy within nature. Since the God she worshipped was the creator of all nature, neither nature as a whole nor any portion of it could be viewed as sacred. Israel denied the existence of the Wintu Indian's spirit of the earth. She accepted all of creation as given to man for his well-being.

Nevertheless, the natural environment was not reduced simply to means. In that first chapter of Genesis, so fateful for the course of human events, God perceives that the subhuman world is good. He sees this quite without reference to man. Its goodness is intrinsic. It shares with man the status of creaturehood. It participates with him in witnessing to God's greatness. Thus when man is freed to govern the world, the world he governs is not thereby reduced to mere means to his end.

Christianity introduces a more radical self-transcendence. The intensification of freedom and individuality that is involved separates man from the subhuman environment even more drastically than did the personal existence of the Jew. At the same time, the contrast between what is and what ought to be, already vividly developed in Jewish apocalypticism, is intensified. Original sin and its cosmic consequences are keenly felt. Man is turned toward God and his fellow man, and his natural environment almost loses significance. What emerges is an extreme humanism, a strong sense of man's deep internality, his infinitely important selfhood, and his radical transcendence over the subhuman world. The profoundly self-conscious

individual could escape the misery of self-preoccupa-
tion only by authentic love of others.

Not only is love essential to the Christian in a
new way, but also the quality of his love is new.
Whereas for the Jew love of neighbor meant justice
and righteousness in the treatment of his neighbor, for
the Christian love of neighbor means an actual concern for him as a fellow human being. Such concern
should express itself in just and righteous treatment,
but it is not motivated by the desire to be righteous.
In that sense it is the motiveless motive of Christian
action. It is directly connected with the absolute valuation of every individual life, which we have recognized
as the foundation of our traditional ideals.

This high valuation of human life in its individuality and particularity is susceptible to two developments in relation to the subhuman world. First, the
focus upon what is distinctively human and inward
tends to widen the gulf between man and other living
things. This can lead, and has indeed led, to the absolutization of this gulf that has dominated modern
Western ideals. The second possible development is
that the concern for others, now directed toward fellow human beings, can be extended to subhuman life
as well. This extension of love has been a subdominant element in the modern West.

In Francis of Assisi and Albert Schweitzer, there is
a disinterested love of nature quite unlike the primitive attitude and going beyond the Old Testament recognition of the goodness of all creation. This love of
nature involves no disparagement of man, for he is the
apex and summation of nature. It need not prevent
man from continuing his scientific investigations of nature. Indeed, it can provide such inquiry with a
deeper motivation, a level of motivation that has been
lacking since the acids of modernity destroyed the vision of divinely imposed order. It need not reject tech-

nological manipulation of the subhuman world where that is needed for the sake of a richer life for man. But it would prevent ruthless indifference to the consequences of our actions for the living environment. Every human action must be measured in terms both of its consequences for man and of its consequences for other living things. That man is of vastly greater worth than any other creature does not reduce the value of the others to nothing.

But Western man has translated this relative superiority into a radical disjunction. Especially since Kant, thinkers have feared that to treat man as part of nature would turn him into a mere object. Such an object would have no intrinsic value or at best no greater value than dogs and cows. But such a fear is ill-founded. By distinguishing within nature the human and the subhuman, we can continue to recognize man's superior value without disparaging or denying the intrinsic value of other living things.

The extension of Christian love beyond man to other living things, which is justified and demanded by this vision, is a continuation and development of our biblical Christian heritage rather than its repudiation. Nevertheless, the Christianity that will emerge is significantly new.

Fuller discussion of the *new* Christianity will be found in the last three chapters of the book. Here, just one topic will be considered—the question of the sacredness or absolute value of *human* life. That human life is an absolute has been the fundamental dogma of the modern West, shared by Christians and non-Christian humanists alike.

The deep-seated sense of something sacred or absolute persists in our highly secularized age, but it is often unrecognized. To bring it to consciousness, let us consider first our attitude toward incest. We can give good pragmatic arguments against sexual intercourse between a son and his mother. Its practice is incompatible with wholesome family life, and there seem to be some genetic disadvantages for the offspring of such unions. But the feelings many people have about incest are disproportionate to its harmfulness. To them it seems absolutely wrong; it would still be wrong even if psychologists, sociologists, and geneticists provided evidence that its widespread practice would be beneficial.

The sense of sacredness or absoluteness attaches not only to ethical principles but more fundamentally to entities. Some hold their country sacred. This attitude is expressed in the common meaning of the saying "My country right or wrong" or, more recently, "America, love it or leave it." These sayings imply that commitment or devotion to one's country does not depend on its contribution to the good of humanity in general or even to its own citizens. It is an absolute. The American who thus views his country as a sacred object judges other nations and individual Americans according to their contributions to the interests of the United States, but he does not judge the United States by any higher norm.

Humanists condemn this idolatrous attitude toward a nation-state. They affirm patriotism, but a man's higher loyalty should be to the good of mankind generally. It is in this object that the humanist finds *his* absolute. To the question of why it is appropriate to serve humanity, there is no answer. Either one recognizes the absolute worth of human beings, individually and collectively, or he does not. The humanist refuses to judge individuals in terms of their contribution to society. Whether or not the individual contributes to the wider community, he is of absolute value in himself. That means human life is sacred.

To view human life as sacred is to believe that

its value is beyond calculation, that it is incommensurate with all other values, and that it should be treated only as an end and never as a means. The inculcation of this view of man, both of oneself and of one's neighbors, has been at the heart of Western moral teaching. Modern ethics, in both its utilitarian and its Kantian forms, take *man's* good as its unquestioned context.

Of course, we have been far from consistent in our affirmation of the sacredness of human personality. We have made official exceptions in the cases of capital punishment and just war. Clearly we have, in fact, calculated about the value of one life in comparison with others. But in spite of these exceptions, the sense of absoluteness with respect to the value of human life has controlled large areas of our attitude and practice.

The influence of this doctrine has been widely beneficial, but we are now recognizing that it has harmful consequences as well. Only one thing can be absolute. If human values are absolute, then other animals have value *only* as they serve human ends. It logically follows that any amount of suffering may be inflicted on animals if the result is some enhancement, even a slight one, of human enjoyment. And practice follows theory: We torture horses, for example, by tightening a strap around their kidneys and intestines so that we can enjoy "bucking broncos" at our rodeos, or by "soreing" their front feet we force them at the price of agony to walk in ways we find entertaining in our horse shows.

Even more seriously, we have seen, the lack of concern for the subhuman world continues to lead to actions that threaten human survival as well. Hence, in order to foster this wider concern, we must challenge and alter the basic principle of humanism itself. The change would be modest if we could simply extend to other forms of life the sacredness attributed to human life. But that is not possible. We can forbid cannibalism, but we cannot forbid the eating of other living things. Even if we insisted on vegetarianism, declaring only animal life sacred, we would still have to kill some animals for the sake of others, or else let all the carnivores in our zoos starve. Schweitzer was forced to kill fish to save the life of a bird.

To choose responsibly we require principles of judgment and calculation that are incompatible with viewing all living things as absolute values. To guide us here Aldo Leopold offers the image of the biotic pyramid beginning with the soil and proceeding through insects, plants, birds, and rodents, to the larger carnivores, and finally to man. Energy from the sun flows upward through the pyramid. "Evolution is a long series of self-induced changes, the net result of which has been to elaborate the flow mechanism and to lengthen the circuit." [2] Thus the evolutionary process, when man does not interfere, works toward maximization of the pyramid by both building the soil and multiplying the variety and complexity of the forms of life it supports.

Man's interference in most places and at most times has reversed this process by impoverishing the soil and reducing the complexity of the biotic pyramid. To extend concern to all living things calls man to work with rather than against the evolutionary process. He must adapt his actions so that both the base and the complexity of the biotic pyramid may again grow, both for man's sake and for the sake of other species of which it is composed.

The new Christianity must substitute a vision of a healthy biotic pyramid with man at its apex

2. *Op. cit.*, p. 254.

for the absoluteness of man. This negation of the sacredness of human life is not without biblical grounds. Indeed, in its purest form prophetic faith has affirmed that only God is sacred or absolute. That doctrine *can* have profoundly negative consequences by reducing man and all creation to mere instruments of God. Humanism has often been justified in criticizing certain types of theism for their depreciation of human value. But if God is understood as concerned for and involved in the whole evolutionary process culminating in man, then these negative consequences can be avoided. In that case, renewal of the biblical vision of God as alone sacred would undergird and direct appropriate action in God's world.

Discussion Questions

1. What kind of goodness in the subhuman world is affirmed by the creation account in Genesis 1?

2. Does man have obligations to other living species? In what sense may they be said to have "rights"?

3. Would we still be Christians if we extended love to all creatures? Why? In what sense can we "love" nonpersonal objects? How does this differ from what we ordinarily mean by love?

4. What do you think of the value of human life? Is capital punishment a violation of the "sacredness" of human life? Can we respect human personality without regarding it as sacred?

absoluteness of man. This negation of the
s of human life is not without biblical
Indeed, in its purest form prophetic faith
ned that only God is sacred or absolute. That
can have profoundly negative consequences
cing man and all creation to mere instru-
f God. Humanism has often been justified
izing certain types of theism for their de-
n of human value. But if God is understood
rned for and involved in the whole evolu-
process culminating in man, then these nega-
sequences can be avoided. In that case, re-
f the biblical vision of God as alone sacred
undergird and direct appropriate action in
orld.

ssion Questions

hat kind of goodness in the subhuman
rld is affirmed by the creation account in
nesis 1?

es man have obligations to other living spe-
s? In what sense may they be said to have
ights"?

ould we still be Christians if we extended
ve to all creatures? Why? In what sense can
e "love" nonpersonal objects? How does this
ffer from what we ordinarily mean by love?
hat do you think of the value of human
fe? Is capital punishment a violation of the
acredness" of human life? Can we respect
uman personality without regarding it as sa-
red?

intercourse between a son and his mother. Its practice is incompatible with wholesome family life, and
there seem to be some genetic disadvantages for the
offspring of such unions. But the feelings many people have about incest are disproportionate to its harmfulness. To them it seems absolutely wrong; it would
still be wrong even if psychologists, sociologists, and
geneticists provided evidence that its widespread practice would be beneficial.

The sense of sacredness or absoluteness attaches
not only to ethical principles but more fundamentally
to entities. Some hold their country sacred. This attitude is expressed in the common meaning of the
saying "My country right or wrong" or, more recently,
"America, love it or leave it." These sayings imply
that commitment or devotion to one's country does
not depend on its contribution to the good of humanity in general or even to its own citizens. It is
an absolute. The American who thus views his country as a sacred object judges other nations and individual Americans according to their contributions to
the interests of the United States, but he does not
judge the United States by any higher norm.

Humanists condemn this idolatrous attitude toward a nation-state. They affirm patriotism, but a
man's higher loyalty should be to the good of mankind generally. It is in this object that the humanist
finds *his* absolute. To the question of why it is appropriate to serve humanity, there is no answer. Either
one recognizes the absolute worth of human beings,
individually and collectively, or he does not. The
humanist refuses to judge individuals in terms of
their contribution to society. Whether or not the individual contributes to the wider community, he is
of absolute value in himself. That means human life
is sacred.

To view human life as sacred is to believe that

its value is beyond calculation, that it is incommensurate with all other values, and that it should be treated only as an end and never as a means. The inculcation of this view of man, both of oneself and of one's neighbors, has been at the heart of Western moral teaching. Modern ethics, in both its utilitarian and its Kantian forms, take *man's* good as its unquestioned context.

Of course, we have been far from consistent in our affirmation of the sacredness of human personality. We have made official exceptions in the cases of capital punishment and just war. Clearly we have, in fact, calculated about the value of one life in comparison with others. But in spite of these exceptions, the sense of absoluteness with respect to the value of human life has controlled large areas of our attitude and practice.

The influence of this doctrine has been widely beneficial, but we are now recognizing that it has harmful consequences as well. Only one thing can be absolute. If human values are absolute, then other animals have value *only* as they serve human ends. It logically follows that any amount of suffering may be inflicted on animals if the result is some enhancement, even a slight one, of human enjoyment. And practice follows theory: We torture horses, for example, by tightening a strap around their kidneys and intestines so that we can enjoy "bucking broncos" at our rodeos, or by "soreing" their front feet we force them at the price of agony to walk in ways we find entertaining in our horse shows.

Even more seriously, we have seen, the lack of concern for the subhuman world continues to lead to actions that threaten human survival as well. Hence, in order to foster this wider concern, we must challenge and alter the basic principle of humanism itself. The change would be modest if we

could simply extend to other
ness attributed to human lif
ble. We can forbid cannibalis
the eating of other living thi
on vegetarianism, declaring c
we would still have to kill sor
of others, or else let all the
starve. Schweitzer was forced t
life of a bird.

To choose responsibly we
judgment and calculation that
viewing all living things as abs
us here Aldo Leopold offers th
pyramid beginning with the
through insects, plants, birds,
larger carnivores, and finally t
the sun flows upward through t
tion is a long series of self-indu
result of which has been to elab
anism and to lengthen the circu
lutionary process, when man does
toward maximization of the pyram
the soil and multiplying the vari
of the forms of life it supports.

Man's interference in most p
times has reversed this process by
soil and reducing the complexity c
mid. To extend concern to all l
man to work with rather than agai
ary process. He must adapt his act
the base and the complexity of th
may again grow, both for man's sake
of other species of which it is composec

The new Christianity must sul
of a healthy biotic pyramid with r

2. *Op. cit.*, p. 254.

for the
sacredn
ground
has aff
doctrin
by rec
ments
in cri
precia
as cor
tionar
tive c
newa
woul
God's

Disc

1.

2.

3.

4.

7

A Style of Life for the Survival of Life

Through much of its history Christianity has advocated asceticism. The sense of the superior importance of spirit in relation to body has led to the attempt to concentrate all attention on perfecting spirit. Concern for the body has sometimes been condemned. It has even been thought that the spirit was directly benefited by denial of the body or even by the imposition of suffering upon it.

We have largely outgrown that kind of asceticism. We recognize more clearly today than in much of our Christian past that spirit and body jointly constitute one person, that both are good, that God is concerned for both, and that it is the total person who is to be forgiven and made whole. We recognize also that the world is good and that its enjoyment is good. Nothing is unclean in itself. God wants happiness and not misery. We particularly realize that the deeply entrenched view of sex as unclean and requiring special conditions for the justification of its practice is false. Sex is, or can be, a good and beautiful part of natural and wholesome life. Justification is required for restrictions placed upon it, not for its free expression.

As the rigors of Christian asceticism subsided, an economic asceticism emerged. It required hard work to earn enough of the world's goods to raise a family. One must work still harder and be even more careful

in his expenditures if he is to save. Only with savings
can he have capital, and only with capital can he advance economically. Hence frugality is a major virtue,
and waste, a major sin.

Those of us who lived through the depression will
readily understand this kind of asceticism. But in the
years since World War II it also has faded in the industrialized world and especially in our own country.
Immense economic expansion has occurred, and its encouragement has been regarded as a major virtue. The
expansion has been based on free borrowing and free
spending on ever new products. Goods are manufac-
tured to last only a few years so that they may be
thrown away and replaced with newer and presumably
better ones. Of course, none of us are ever able to buy
all that we would like to own. Hence few of us feel
fully part of the community of affluence. But almost
all of us are spending freely on goods we would have
learned to do without in the years of depression and
World War II. In this context, economic asceticism is
no longer a virtue. At most it is an occasional necessity imposed on some of us from time to time.

But as we face the fact of the finitude of the
world's resources and the frightening pollution that is
being caused by the present pace of production and
consumption, we must move forward to a new asceticism, an ecological asceticism. We must find ways of
reducing our destruction of the environment and of
making irreplaceable resources last longer. Where
shall we begin?

The obvious place to begin is with war and the
preparation for war. From an ecological point of view
nothing is more wasteful and destructive. Indeed, it is
our preparations for war that have most clearly
brought the whole question of survival to the fore. If
we could reduce by half the production of war material, destroy all of our apocalyptic weapons, and cease

to use our destructive power on the people and land of Southeast Asia, we would make immense strides toward bringing our national consumption of the world's resources and our national contribution to the destruction of the planet within reasonable limits.

But much, much more than this must be done. One large area is that of transportation. Our present system of transportation, in which we use two or three hundred horse power to transport one or two people everywhere they go, hastens the exhaustion of irreplaceable resources of gasoline and iron, poisons the air we breathe so that even plants cannot survive, and adds massively to the problem of disposal of solid wastes. Something drastic must be done quickly. Those of us who live in Southern California have already lost an average of a year or two from our lives because of the smog we breathe. The rest of the nation is not far behind.

Obviously much can be done. The Europeans and Japanese have long showed us how we can transport ourselves only a little less luxuriously with much less gasoline. But Detroit has largely ignored this possibility, and it is too late now for such halfway measures. We must either ban the internal combustion engine or achieve technical miracles in its performance, which until recently Detroit was not even willing to attempt. Meanwhile, we must make private transportation unattractive in relation to public transportation. This can be done by heavily taxing the former and heavily subsidizing the latter. An additional thirty percent tax on private automobiles and on gas, combined with turning freeways into toll ways, would raise enough money in California to provide comfortable and rapid public transportation. This should be inexpensive or even free. We could then almost stop construction of new highways. These may sound like drastic steps. But they are in fact very moderate in relation to the problem.

We also need to go into a new kind of city planning based on proximity of residence, work, and shopping, convenient public transportation, the encouragement of walking and bicycle riding, and the virtual elimination of private automobiles. New construction should be built upward on land already committed to housing, and further inroads on agricultural and wilderness lands should virtually cease. We should experiment with the mile-high cities envisioned by Paolo Soleri.

With regard to our irreplaceable resources, a strict policy on lumbering should be instituted to insure that no further reduction of forests be tolerated and that substantial reforestration occur every year. If this leads to shortages of wood and wood products, these should not be made up by imports. On the contrary, the price of such products should rise sufficiently to discourage their use and to encourage recycling. Similarly, irreplaceable metals should be heavily taxed to discourage their use and encourage the development of substitutes. In general, the cost of new products in relation to repairs on old ones should be increased. The cost of water and electricity should also be increased to the point where we would all be less wasteful.

Since it seems likely that large agricultural surpluses will be needed in the years ahead to meet crises in Latin America, Africa, and Asia, full scale production should be encouraged. However, this should be done with drastically reduced use of insecticides and chemical fertilizers. If this reduces yield per acre, so be it. New methods of farming less dependent on chemicals can be devised. Temporary shortages will not be critical in comparison with the devastation that continued indiscriminate use of chemicals can work. Most of us could tighten our belts a little without damage to our health.

If you think that these proposals would raise costs without raising salaries, you are quite right. That is part of the purpose. If we can afford to buy less, we will do without. Especially, we can do without automobiles. But we could also reduce our present consumption of water, electricity, metal, and wood products. If repair shops were available we could continue to use many of the appliances we now discard in favor of new ones. Life would not be unbearable!

There should be a quick end to what we now know as garbage collection. In its place would be a system of separate collections of each type of waste that can be recycled or converted into organic fertilizer. Such collection should be free. On the other hand, a high charge should be placed on the disposal of unusable waste.

Some system must be devised for encouraging industry to concentrate on the production of high quality, long lasting, easily repaired goods rather than to continue the present planned obsolescence. The whole system of new styles, and of advertising intended to create dissatisfaction with serviceable equipment, must be discouraged and resisted.

All of this would cause some economic dislocation, and the easing of hardships caused thereby should be a major national priority. Total production for the private sector would be somewhat reduced, although the higher quality demanded and the increased emphasis on repairs could prevent reduction in the number of men employed. There would be ample place for the exertion of energies diverted from overproduction. Enormous expenditures will be necessary. It will be extremely costly in goods and services merely to stop the increase of pollution of our waterways. To clear up those already polluted will cost more.

In this country, my proposals would lead to considerable reduction in the consumption of petroleum products and some reduction in the consumption of electricity. They also would require relative stability of consumption in other industrialized nations. This would enable these countries to convert gradually and cautiously to the use of other sources of energy as the supply of fossil fuels declines. Use of atomic energy should be expanded only if more adequate provisions can be made for disposition of wastes and heat. The use of solar energy, geothermal energy, and energy from ocean waves appears to be ecologically safer. If we can experiment without the pressure of urgency, safe long-term sources of energy may be harnessed.

It may be too much to hope that the underindustrialized nations will be cautious about the ecological consequences of their development. We can hardly ask these nations to husband resources carefully after the pattern of exploitation we have set. Even so, if we begin to set a new example ourselves and to be more generous and wise in our assistance, improvement is possible.

While affluent Americans learn to consume less, levels of consumption in some segments of American society should be increased. Shifting from expensive private cars to subsidized public transportation would be one step toward improving the lot of the poor. But much else must be done.

Whereas in the past we have employed our surplus wealth for industrial expansion and the purchase of additional goods, we should now put the emphasis on services. We have been voting down money for schools so as to buy a second car, or add a backyard swimming pool, or redecorate our homes. We must reverse this. Education is ecologically cheap. We should refrain from further expansion of our total industrial plant and put our resources instead into improving the ratio of teachers to students in our schools. Especially the children of the disadvantaged should be pro-

vided with numerous well-paid teachers. These should
be given all possible encouragement by the community to experiment with ways of overcoming these
children's handicaps. We can expand work in the
mental health field as well. The arts also should be
subsidized and encouraged. In all these areas services
should be free or inexpensive. If we must learn gradually to be satisfied with fewer and less elegant goods,
we can reasonably ask that these be replaced with services designed to enrich the life of the mind, deepen
self-understanding, and improve human relations. Rev-
enue from the high taxes designed to discourage waste
of metals, wood products, electricity, and water can
subsidize education, mental health, and the arts.

I introduced this discussion by speaking of a
new, ecological asceticism. Yet the style of life I have
sketched is hardly ascetic by past standards. Indeed,
viewed in perspective, the change from the present affluent life is not immense. We could make these
changes if we wanted.

The real question is whether they would be sufficient. They would certainly slow down our consumption of irreplaceable resources, make possible some increase in recreational lands, forests, and wilderness,
and greatly reduce pollution. But the remaining rate
of consumption would still involve ecologically harmful practices, and irreplaceable resources would still
be used in large quantity. More drastic measures
might be required.

This chapter has considered the American situation. Most of the other industrial nations may not
need to reduce so greatly their level of consumption,
but changes will be required of all of them. Their
major need may be only to abandon their visions of a
continuing increase in production. Something near the
present level of economic activity in Japan and Europe might serve as a satisfactory norm for the long

term. The world's task, its Herculean labor, is to bring the unindustrialized nations up toward this standard of life. This *cannot* be accomplished unless population is stabilized or reduced. Even then it *may* be impossible without ecological catastrophe. But we must try. A stable and generous America could do much to help.

Discussion Questions

1. What are the reasons for ecological asceticism?
2. What shape should ecological asceticism take? Is it possible or desirable that the measures described in this chapter be taken? Have you any better suggestions?
3. Is it wise to use taxing powers for ecological purposes?
4. Is ecological asceticism possible without international cooperation and control? How could this be arranged?

8

Too Many People—the Ethical Problem

When it comes to proposals like those in the previous chapter, there will certainly be objections. Some will regard them as unrealistic and excessive. Some will oppose the further restrictions on laissez-faire capitalism. Others will regard them as entirely insufficient and far too moderate in their implications for our economic system. But few would oppose them as immoral or incompatible with fundamental ethical principles.

However, none of our efforts will be of much avail unless the total population of the nation is stabilized. Suppose that by measures of the sort suggested, we succeeded over a twenty-year period in reducing per capita consumption of goods (not services) by twenty-five percent. This would require somewhat more than a twenty-five percent decrease on the part of the majority to allow for a very much needed increase on the part of the now underprivileged. That would be an impressive achievement when we consider that it would require a reversal of all existing trends! Nevertheless, a modest population growth of just over one percent annually would wipe it out. Our total national consumption of the earth's resources in 1990 would still be at its present ecologically unacceptable level.

On the other hand, if we did reduce our per capita consumption while stabilizing our population, we could both improve our environment and make major contributions to other peoples in their struggle to achieve a decent mode of life. In the nonindustrialized countries we could give priority to programs designed to achieve population stability and in some cases reductions. If this occurred, then twenty years from now the planet might not be twenty years nearer the extinction of life but instead be moving toward an era of stability and a balance with the environment that might endure. Surely the latter is the more attractive prospect.

But talk of population stability has profound moral implications. Some who think of each individual human life as having absolute value believe that the more lives the better. For them, the quality of the individual life is a secondary consideration. That is an extreme view. But even if few advocate it in just those terms, it influences the thought of many. If it is correct, then we should seek the largest possible population for the planet, be indifferent to the extermination of other forms of life, and accept the relative misery of the crowded individuals. If a man holds to this principle, we can only deter him from pushing for rapidly increasing population by showing that this backfires, that the attempt to increase the population will bring on wars, famines, and pestilences that will in fact reduce it. And if he believes that God or nature is on the side of such increase he will be even more difficult to convince. He will expect the unexpected. He may even talk of peopling other planets as our vocation!

To one who thinks in these terms there is no moral justification for discouraging or preventing births. In his view the attempt to do so expresses a selfish desire to enjoy the economic advantages and personal freedom that small families make possible. Or else it expresses a fundamental failure to appreciate the absolute value of human life and the accompanying reduction of all other things to their instrumental value.

Action expressing these principles would be self-defeating. Man does not have the choice of rapid increase of population over a long period of time. The planet cannot support him. More people can survive longer if measures are taken promptly to prevent such increase of population. The importance of the vision within which one operates appears again at this point. One who believes in population growth as a good for its own sake will yield on each point only when it is unequivocally necessary to do so. Compromise of that sort will inevitably be too little and too late.

The alternative principle to which I have appealed is the reverence for all life. Those who live by this vision will seek a balance and harmony between as many forms of life as possible. Of course they will unhesitatingly choose human life over any other form when the choice is to be made. But they will favor restraint on man's part. The annihilation of other species need not occur so frequently. Men can work with the total movement of life on the planet rather than destroy all but the human portion and that most obviously necessary to man. Birth control will be the single most important expression of the needed restraint.

Birth control can be encouraged in many ways. Women must be given opportunities for fulfilling vocations other than motherhood. Sex education should be mandatory in our schools. A social stigma would be attached to large families in the future. Contraceptives should be cheap and accessible. Tax laws should make more than two children financially unattractive. Once we have accepted the moral importance of stabilizing population, such measures will be clearly appropriate.

From a practical point of view, in an industrialized nation these are the most important measures.

But in this chapter we are focusing on ethical issues and their relation to basic conviction, attitude, or consciousness. In this connection, the issue of abortion is especially important and interesting. It is not without its practical importance for controlling population. It has been extensively used in Japan and Eastern European countries in their successful efforts to limit population and it may be necessary elsewhere. Even in our nation, although other means will play the dominant role, abortion may also be important. There are still hundreds of thousands of unplanned and unwanted babies born in the United States every year. Legal, inexpensive abortions will help to reduce that number.

Recently the argument for abortion has centered around the rights of the mother. Should the state force a woman to carry to term an unwanted child? Only now is the further question being asked: To help achieve population stability should society discourage the bearing of unwanted children?

One way of approaching such a question is purely pragmatic and social. We might assume that the end to be sought is a smoothly functioning and happy society. We might then decide on policies with respect to abortion solely in terms of their contribution to this end. However, such a position would violate strong convictions about what is right and wrong. These include elements of absoluteness that stand in tension with purely pragmatic considerations about the welfare of society.

The idea of something being absolute was introduced in Chapter 6. There "absolute" was treated as the secular equivalent of "sacred." When something is viewed as sacred, or as absolute in this sense, it is excluded from evaluation in terms of further consequences.

In the dominant Western tradition the destruction of a fetus is absolutely wrong *if* the fetus is "human." But how can one decide when the organism becomes "human"? Some have suggested that it is human when it is first capable of life separate from the mother. Others date the humanity from quickening. Still others have pushed back the date to conception itself. But all such decisions are arbitrary, since there are no sudden breaks or abrupt departures in the development from fertilization to birth.

The problem can be solved by a step that was proposed in Chapter 6. If we give up the sense of absoluteness or sacredness with respect to human life, the question of when the fetus becomes human is no longer decisive. We are free to adjust our view of the humanity of the organism to the evidence and state that the process of development is one in which distinctively human traits gradually emerge both in the womb and after birth. Then, although by some definitions the unfertilized ovum is already human and by others even a saint is not yet fully human, such diversity of definitions will be acceptable because no moral absolutes hinge upon discovering the *true* or *correct* definition. If the human is not sacred or absolute, then the prohibition against taking innocent human life is not absolute either. That it is worse to destroy a child ready to be born than a newly fertilized ovum is not denied, but this now becomes a matter of degree.

Earlier I contrasted our tendency to see some moral principles as absolute with a vaguely indicated norm of social welfare. One profound danger of liberating ourselves from absolutes is that we may then allow the good of society to become the sole criterion of right and wrong. The worth and rights of the individual are then subordinated to the society, and the individual is judged in terms of instrumental value to the whole. If the society finds some of its members undesirable it is then morally free to liquidate them. In that direction lie the gas chambers of Dachau.

Fortunately, we need not and should not choose

between treating individuals as absolute and subordinating the individual to the societal good. The alternative to this choice can be stated in the distinction between intrinsic and instrumental value. Something has intrinsic value when its existence is good in itself, that is, regardless of any consequences or uses it may have for others. In this sense, a joyful experience is intrinsically valuable. A pencil, on the other hand, has negligible intrinsic value. Its existence matters very little apart from its use. The pencil has instrumental value, that is, it helps men to achieve greater intrinsic values.

The joyous experience is not only an intrinsic value; it also has instrumental value. It may have a beneficial effect on subsequent bodily health. It is likely to make one, for a time, a pleasanter companion. It enriches subsequent experiences through being remembered. In such ways every intrinsic value also has instrumental value, but many instrumental values have negligible intrinsic value.

Intrinsic value can be found in experience and experience alone. Generally, Westerners have supposed that it is found only in *human* experience. Against this limitation I have argued above and will argue further. But the limitation of intrinsic value to experience is sound, and experience always belongs to someone or something. Hence society as a whole, or the state, has instrumental value only. It is to be judged as it contributes to the increase of intrinsic value in the actual experiences it affects. To transpose absolute value from individual human beings to a corporate body like the state is, therefore, in no way justified by the general rejection of absolutes. On the contrary, individuals are the one locus of intrinsic value, and the state is to be judged by its contribution to them.

Corresponding to the idea of intrinsic value as

distinct from absolute value is the idea of principles that always have moral weight when they are applicable. Telling the truth is an example. In making an ethical decision as to what to say, one cannot ignore his obligation to tell the truth. But if he must lie to save an innocent human life, then the principle that innocent people are to be saved may well outweigh the other. On the other hand, if he could save an innocent human life only at the expense of condemning many to misery, another principle about enhancing the wider good might outweigh it. In these examples no one principle is absolute; all have intrinsic validity.

The principle that innocent human life should be preserved is a special case, as Schweitzer says, of the principle that all life should be saved. This is certainly not an absolute principle. But it means that no life should be destroyed idly or without cause. Thus there is an important ethical principle counting against the destruction of a fetus at any stage in its development whether or not the most useful definitions of "human" include it. This means that to consider *only* the casual preference of the mother or some slight benefit to society at large as grounds for destruction of a fetus is to violate the principle.

But there are also other principles. The mother's happiness or the general advantages for people not directly involved should *also* be considered. To consider *only* the principle of saving life would violate these and other important principles. The complexity of moral decision results from the complexity of relations among the many principles that demand consideration. None of these principles are absolute. When the situation is viewed in the light of the dangers to all the higher forms of life that result from planetary overpopulation, the outcome of responsible moral reflection will sometimes be more favorable to abortion than when this factor is left out of account.

However, there is an important practical argument against shifting the ethical consideration of abortion from the realm of absolutes to the realm of weighing conflicting valid principles. The taboo on the destruction of innocent human life from conception to natural death has served Western man well. It has given more people more security in their persons than any other society has enjoyed. Its extension around the world has been in most respects a blessing, despite the population explosion to which it has contributed. If the taboo is removed at one point, how can it be held at others? If a fetus may be destroyed, may not an unwanted newborn child also be killed, especially if it is deformed or diseased? Will not euthanasia be approved and the efforts to keep the aged alive relaxed? What about the insane and the hopelessly ill? Finally, what about all those who are a drain on society and those whose genetic contribution to the race is undesirable? If there are too many people, can we not reduce the population selectively in favor of the healthy and intelligent?

Each of these questions has to be faced seriously, but this is not the place. Certainly the removal of an absolute taboo could have many bad consequences. It could lead to casual indifference to individual human life, whereas what we need is much more sensitive concern for the individual than we now show. One reason for urging population stabilization is that if the total population becomes too great this concern for individual life will be further weakened. Men will be viewed more and more as ciphers and less and less as persons.

To avoid the dangerous consequences, we need to emphasize another principle. Every man should be assured of the support of his community in living as long as he desires to live. Of course, that is not an absolute principle either. There seem to be times when killing a man who desires to live is justified. But we should require a great deal of justification before destroying the life of one who wants to live, more justification than is now required, and not less. Our task is to undergird and deepen a genuinely personal concern for each individual without absolute taboos.

Discussion Questions

1. Is population control necessary?
2. How do you think a stable population could be achieved? Which methods of birth control would be acceptable to you? Why?
3. Why not kill unwanted children or adults, especially if they are deformed, diseased, poor, or from other nations or races?
4. What is the basis of the human right to life? Is this right absolute? Does a fetus have a right to live?

PART TWO

The New Vision We Need

9

Nature as Historic

John F. Kennedy wrote: "For the first century after independence, we regarded the natural environment as indestructible—and proceeded vigorously to destroy it." [1] The struggle to change that attitude, and thus to reverse that practice, is far from completed.

In the preceding chapters I described the objective problem we face and some of the steps needed to deal with it. Again and again it was made clear that we must not merely do different things, but must also regard the natural environment in a new way, adopt a fresh attitude, and alter the principles in terms of which we make our decisions.

But we cannot make these changes by a simple act of will. We cannot simply *decide* to love subhuman entities. We can do so only if these entities appear to us as appropriate objects of love. As yet, most expressions of love toward the subhuman world seem naive and sentimental. To enter into those expressions ourselves goes against deeply ingrained habits and fundamental assumptions. It goes against our basic vision of reality.

Consider, for example, how we feel about the two men mentioned in Chapter 6 as embodying the new Christianity we need to adopt. Francis of Assisi is

1. "Introduction," Udall, *op. cit.*, pp. xi–xii.

greatly admired throughout Christendom, but we smile condescendingly at his behavior toward birds and animals. Schweitzer is widely recognized as one of the great men of the twentieth century, but we are a little embarrassed by just that behavior of his which shows that he took seriously the principle of reverence for all life. We tolerate these strange actions as the pardonable foibles of a saint and genius.

As long as our vision remains estranged from theirs, it is useless to pretend to adopt their attitudes. If we do not see the subhuman world as real and valuable in its own right, to love it is sentimental nonsense. The remainder of this chapter and the next three are devoted to overcoming elements in the orthodox view that block disinterested concern for the subhuman world.

The universe is mostly a vast, almost empty, expanse of space-time. Scattered through it in an uneven but not quite random way are innumerable stars. Around some of these revolve satellites that we call planets. One of these planets revolving around a star of modest size is alive. We call that planet Earth.

Perhaps there are other living planets circling other stars in this or other galaxies. But the conditions requisite for any high grade of life to appear are far more special and complex than is often recognized. A planet must be neither too large nor too small, neither too heavy nor too light, and neither too close nor too distant from its star. Its development must occur in a definite and by no means inevitable sequence. Suitable mutations must appear at particular times.

Even if life has appeared elsewhere in the universe, it is highly unlikely that it has used the same amino acids or the same genetic code. Even if somewhere it has chanced to do so, there is no reason to suppose that it would have followed a line of development culminating in creatures similar to man. There is no necessity in the emergence of mammals or primates. There is nothing about primates that insures the evolutionary emergence of man. The primates of the New World would never have evolved in this way.

The other planets in our solar system are presumed lifeless. We know nothing of life elsewhere in the universe. In an area to be measured by hundreds of light years, if not in all the infinities of space, we are alone.

This planet has not always been alive. Indeed, as Richard Overman [2] has recently reminded us, if we conceive the five billion years of the Earth's past as though recorded in ten volumes of five hundred pages each, so that each page records a million years, cellular life appears only somewhere around the eighth volume, about a billion years ago. The story of all the plants and animals of the Cambrian period occupies only the tenth volume, and of this, the first half is taken up with how plants became terrestrial and the amphibians emerged. Around page 440 of this 500-page book the reptiles reach the height of their development, and it is not until page 465 that their dominance is superseded by that of birds and warm-blooded animals. Finally, on page 499 of this tenth volume man appears. The last two words on the last page recount his story from the rise of civilization six thousand years ago until the present.

Throughout the last two volumes life proliferated, creating an environment in which more complex forms of life could emerge and prosper. Both life and the capacity to support life increased millennia after millennia. Man entered the scene on a planet that was biologically very rich indeed. To that organic richness he contributed little. In fact, in certain localities over

2. "A Christological View of Nature," *Religious Education* LXVI, January–February 1971, p. 37.

limited periods of time his treatment of his environment was quite destructive. But only when we reach
the last letter of the last word on the last page does he
turn the tide against life. Only then does man begin
the process of killing the planet. What is astonishing
is that all that has been produced over the course
of a billion years is so vulnerable to destruction by
this late-latecomer to the scene.

Yet it should not surprise us that what takes so
long to create can be so easily destroyed. It took only
a moment for an assassin's bullet to destroy the complex richness of the life of a John F. Kennedy or a
Martin Luther King. That richness of thought, will,
and feeling had been many years in the making, but it
depended on an organic base that could be destroyed
almost instantaneously. The life of the planet similarly
depends on a physical base which, now that its secrets
have been mastered by man, is vulnerable to his destruction. For at least a hundred years, and with ever-
quickening acceleration, we have been destroying it.
The eleventh volume may recount the much poorer
story of a lifeless planet.

This perspective on ourselves is important because of the profound illusions we Westerners, and especially we Americans, have entertained about our
natural environment. We have supposed, consciously
or unconsciously, that it is inexhaustible and indestructible. Of course, we have known that a few species
of wildlife were becoming extinct and that here and
there we had turned fertile fields into dust bowls, but
these we felt were isolated phenomena having nothing
to do with our basic situation. We thought that we
could learn lessons from our mistakes and through
ever-increasing scientific knowledge and technological
skill advance to new heights of prosperity and comfort.
We might worry about the loss of some prized moral
and spiritual values, but our pictures of future life

were always in terms of fantastic progress in science and technology. In this scenario, nature was cast in the role of supplier of limitless resources for our use and enjoyment.

Now we are discovering that our assault upon nature, intended to wrest from it the materials for this technological utopia, is profoundly affecting her ability to serve us. Even with quite modest technology, ancient man turned fertile land into the Sahara and Gobi deserts. Only an axe is required to expose forest soils to erosion and begin the all too rapid process of creating new wastelands. But today's science and technology introduce whole new means of changing the environment, and their results are far more rapid and drastic. Our means of producing the vast quantities of energy we need both heat and pollute the atmosphere in ways that may either bring on a new ice age or melt the Arctic ice. Our poisons, such as DDT, may kill birds and fish and even plankton, thereby disrupting the ecological cycles on which man, too, ultimately depends. Increase of radiation from the production of atomic energy, even without an atomic war, may alter the genetic character of many species of life including the human. Should another major war occur, it is human and animal life as such, and not merely its quality and character, that is threatened.

Our resistance to the full assimilation of these now well-known facts still stems in large part from our intellectual habits. Especially in Protestant circles, we have been taught to distinguish and contrast history and nature. In history, we suppose, things happen uniquely and irreversibly, whereas in nature they recur and repeat themselves endlessly. Thus history is the only locus of real change. Nature, we assume, will always be the same. In this view, the human, historical future is uncertain, but there is nothing to be anxious about so far as nature is concerned. It is infinite and eternal.

This dualism stems from the distinction between the two modes of investigation. The historian has concerned himself with a narrative account of a sequence of unique and unrepeatable events. The scientist has sought laws which would hold good for all times and places. Yet even this distinction is grossly exaggerated. There are genetic sciences like geology as well as those seeking universal laws. And historians can and do make generalizations about nations, revolutions, and economic depressions.

Aldo Leopold has shown us that human history is itself deeply affected by a biotic succession man does not intend or control. When the forests of Kentucky were cut down, the lush bluegrass appeared. The settlers prospered. But when the American southwest was deforested and grazed, it became barren. Many of the settlers were forced to move on in order to survive. Thus the history of man and that of other forms of life are intertwined.

Yet contrary to all evidence, we have viewed the subhuman world as existing solely for us—a fundamentally inexhaustible and changeless stage on which we are to play out our human drama. We have simply refused to see that the stage participates in the drama, and we are still reluctant to admit that it is beginning to collapse irreparably. Our exaggerated distinction between methods of inquiry in science and history has misled us into supposing that their objects—"natural" and "human" events—are fundamentally distinct and separable.

In this respect, the biblical vision was more accurate than the dominant modern one. The subhuman world, although pictured on a smaller scale still appeared vast to ancient man. It was intimately involved in human history, sharing in man's fall, suffering from his sin, and destined to share redemption in the end.

Today we would picture man's role in the cosmic drama as important only in its very latest stages. But

that the subhuman world, too, has a history, and that
this history is intimately bound up with that of man
so that they will suffer a common fate, is all too
sadly true.

This view of nature as historic and contingent
helps to awaken us to the full seriousness of the problem that we now face. It has another importance as
well. It brings the subhuman world closer to us so that
by seeing how our fates are bound up together, by recognizing how much we are indebted to it and depend
upon it, and by realizing how vulnerable it is to our
actions and how deeply we have wounded it, we enter
into a new consciousness. That consciousness nurtures
warmer and more tender feelings. When we view living nature in all its innumerable forms as sharing
with us in a precarious existence, and when we see the
products of aeons of struggle threatened with extinction, we can no longer be indifferent.

Discussion Questions

1. Is a sharp distinction between history and
   nature possible? Is it desirable?
2. How must the recognition of nature's history
   change our attitude toward it?
3. How are nature and man interrelated?

I0

Man as Part of Nature

In every religion what is sought with the help of the
superhuman spiritual power reverenced by man, is a
solution of the contradiction in which man finds himself, as both a part of the world of nature and a spiritual
personality claiming to dominate nature. . . . In this
juncture, religion springs up as faith in superhuman
spiritual powers, by whose help the power which man
possesses of himself is in some way supplemented, and
elevated into a unity of its own kind which is a match
for the pressure of the natural world.[1]

So wrote Albrecht Ritschl, the most influential
Protestant theologian of the latter part of the nineteenth century. For him nature was something that
pressed upon man, something that man was called
upon to dominate. The function of religion was to assist in achieving this dominance. This separation of
man from the rest of nature and this fundamentally
negative attitude toward nature were all too typical of
Protestant theology up to the time when awareness of
the ecological crisis dawned.

One of the first theological books to be stimulated
by the awareness of this crisis was Frederick Elder's

1. Albrecht B. Ritschl, *The Christian Doctrine of Justification and Reconciliation,* 2d ed., trans. H. R. Mackin-
tosh and A. B. Macaulay (Edinburgh: T. & T. Clark, 1902),
p. 199.

Crisis in Eden. Elder sees one main theological issue, that is, the choice between the view of those like Ritschl whom he calls exclusionists and that of the inclusionists whom he supports. Exclusionists view man as outside of nature and in opposition to it. Inclusionists see man as within and part of nature.

Because the word nature has so rich a history and so varied a range of connotations, I have spoken often of the subhuman world instead. Obviously, by definition, man is external to the subhuman world, but that by no means settles the issue Elder is raising. That issue is how man is related to the subhuman world. Does he see himself as separated from it by a radical discontinuity, or does he see himself as continuous with it? Does he see his relation to everything else as fundamentally of a different order from the relation of other things to each other, or does he see his relation to the subhuman world as a special case of the kinds of relations that exist within that world?

As examples of exclusionists, Elder uses his Harvard teachers Herbert Richardson and Harvey Cox. His example of an inclusionist is Loren Eiseley. It is instructive that he went outside the professional theological community to find an inclusionist. I wish that this had been unnecessary, that he could have chosen a theological naturalist. But the Christian tradition has been deeply committed to the exclusionist view.

I align myself with the inclusionists for two reasons. First, they are factually correct. Man evolved with and from the subhuman world, and although he has crossed many thresholds in his development, none of them constitutes the sort of divide that would justify the exclusionist view. Man's difference from a chimpanzee is analogous to a chimpanzee's difference from a sardine or a sardine's difference from an amoeba. These differences are vast, but they do not justify views of total discontinuity when the evidence of evolutionary continuity is so great.

Since most exclusionists today acknowledge the evolutionary connection, the factual argument is not to be pressed. But whereas they think that the fact of evolution is not important for man's fundamental self-understanding, it seems to me of great importance. They focus attention on some special aspect of man, such as his reason, his self-consciousness, or his speech. They hold that however this came into being, it now marks man off decisively from all other forms of life. The factual question between us, then, is the separability of that distinctive aspect of man from the rest of his being and its discontinuity with the subhuman world. Here the argument is often complex and dependent on philosophical assumptions.

Therefore it will be better to stress my second reason for favoring inclusionism which is that it will further that next step in the development of Christian existence for which I called in Chapter 6. There I suggested that whereas Christianity has thus far urged us to have concern for all our fellow human beings, we need now to extend our concern to the whole of life. Only if we do this will we take those actions which will insure our own survival.

As Christians we speak more often of love than of concern or reverence. But there are many kinds of love. Within the family there is the love between husband and wife, the love between parents and children, and the love among the children. Freud has taught us to recognize an erotic element in all human relations, but this is most clearly and best symbolized in the love between husband and wife. This kind of love has played a large role in man's religions and it is affirmed and approved by Christianity. But it is not the kind of love we are called to extend to all human beings and beyond. This universal love is better symbolized as brotherly love. In the ideal relation between brothers there is no possessiveness or attempt to achieve intense feelings of relatedness. There is an ac-

ceptance of the brother as a fellow human being who
is to go his own way as a quite separate and independent person. But there is also concern for his welfare
and recognition of responsibility to him and for him.

Christianity has accentuated the nonerotic character of the love for which it calls by stressing that it is
to be directed especially toward the unattractive and
unworthy. Jesus sought out the sick and the sinner
rather than the healthy and the virtuous. It is not
erotic attractiveness, but need, that governs the direction of active concern. Christian love does not seek to
unite with its objects or to possess them. It seeks their
good for their own sake and encourages their free and
independent development.

But the image of brotherly love also indicates that
Christian love is based on a sense of similarity. The
other is to be loved because he, like myself, is a real
subject of feeling and action. In and of himself he has
the same claim to respect and concern as I have. To
measure him in terms of his value to me is to ignore
the reality in which I believe.

The sense of sharing a common status with all
other men is fundamental to our Christian perspective. But in the past, it has tended to mark off the
boundary of brotherhood at the line dividing man
from other animals. The recognition of kinship has
been limited to the human race. Since it is so difficult
to make effective even this humanly inclusive sense of
kinship against the pressures of racism and national-
ism, the issue of its extension has rarely been raised.

Now, however, it is important for us to extend the
range of respect and concern to subhuman forms of
life. But we cannot simply do this as an act of will.
We can do it only as our vision, our sense of reality,
changes. This will change only as we become vividly
aware of our kinship with other living things. We
must come to experience ourselves as a part of that

whole community of living things to which we point by speaking of the evolutionary process.

There is as much ground for inclusionism as for exclusionism in the Bible. The fateful story of creation represents man as created like the rest, from the dust of the earth. He is cocreature with fish and birds and beasts. The fundamental duality lies between creator and creature, not between man and other animals.

Yet the story speaks of God creating man in his image, thus lifting him above the rest, and Christian theology has focused more upon the image of God in man than upon man's cocreaturehood with other animals. It has given to the idea of the divine image in man a prominence far greater than it is accorded in the Old Testament. It has thus led to a three-fold distinction of God, man, and nature against the more basic biblical distinction of creator and creation. It is the image of cocreaturehood which we need now to recover without the loss of the biblical sense of man as the apex of creation.

In calling for Christians to take seriously man's inclusion within nature, I have implied that few theologians have done so. Yet much recent theology has stressed man's bodiliness. It has opposed no less earnestly than I the dualism that treated man as a purely mental being somehow connected with a piece of machinery that he owns and operates. Indeed, in contemporary theology it has become fashionable to assert that a man *is* his body. This doctrine seems quite close to the stressing of man's inclusion within nature. Just for this reason, the differences are important for the argument of this book. From the perspective of an inclusionist, I have two major objections to offer to the idea that a man is his body. Explaining them will help to make clearer what is involved and what is not involved in inclusionism.

The first objection to the doctrine that a man is

his body is that if it were taken literally and seriously, the value and truth of the historic idea of the soul would be lost. If a man quite unequivocally were his body, then he would be his corpse as well. However, those who adhere to this doctrine do not mean anything of this sort. For them, man is his body functioning in all the dimensions in which the human body can function.

But even when in fairness we allow this qualification to be made, the doctrine is a dangerous one. If it means anything at all, then the excellence of the body and its functioning must be the basis on which men are rightly evaluated. The crippled and the blind are really inferior human beings. In so far as the body structures of various races are significantly different, the people belonging to those races are significantly different.

But these are not the consequences which the doctrine intends to support. Those who say that they *are* their bodies are stressing that they fully accept their bodiliness, refuse to treat their bodily needs and pleasures as inferior to other functions of their person, and give up all thought of a life beyond death separate from their bodies. But if their doctrine is accepted, the unintended consequences follow too—a doctrine is not innocent of its unintended consequences. If we really identify people as bodies, we will and should treat them as such. We will no longer attribute to them the kind of value we have accorded them in the past. There will be no basis for loving them unless we find their bodies and their actions attractive. There will be no idea of a deeper unity transcending differences of appearance. There will be no sense of the possibility of triumphing spiritually over the adversities of the body. Only if we distinguish a feeling and acting subject from the body and its behavior can we distinguish the worth of the person from the attractiveness or excellence of the body. Only then can we conceive the possibility that a cripple may be a better man than a beautiful athlete. Only then can we hold on to the lesson taught mankind by Socrates.

To see man as fully a part of nature does not entail these consequences. If nature were composed only of bodies, of course these results would follow. But nature contains many living beings that feel and act. Man is not alone in being a feeling and acting subject who feels and acts through his body without simply being his body. Man *is* alone in many of the dimensions of his feeling and acting, but his distinctiveness is that of a unique being within nature, not of a being outside nature.

The second objection is that the doctrine that man is his body assumes that the body is more unified in itself and separate from other things than it really is. When one takes this position he does not notice all the ways man's body is involved with its environment. We appreciate man's interconnection with the natural environment only when we see the body as something complex and distinct from the person.

The distinctness of a person from his body does not imply the kind of separateness and difference that Greeks and Christians have often affirmed. The evidence points to a relation that is far more intimate than that. A man's personal life grows out of his body and its experiences, and it expresses itself through the body. A person does not exist before his body or apart from his body. What he is as an experiencing and deciding subject, he is in intimate interrelation with his body. But discrimination is required. His relation to his toenails is quite different from his relation to his liver. His relation to his eyes differs from both. His relation to a red corpuscle in his blood differs from his relation to a cancer cell in his chest or urine in his bladder. Most intimate is his relation to his brain.

That these differences exist can easily be shown physiologically. A local anaesthetic can alter the relation of the person to certain parts of his body. Also, the person is not much changed when his appendix is removed or when he gives blood to the Red Cross. But he is profoundly changed if a substantial part of his brain is removed. These facts seem too obvious to mention. We may be told that a man's self-identification with his body has nothing to do with physiology. But against the unclarified doctrine of indiscriminate identity of person and body, a reminder is needed. A person is intimately involved with his body, but the degree of intimacy with different parts of his body differs. He is not his body as such or in general.

Only when we recognize the diversity of relations within the body are we able to recognize adequately the continuity between a person's relations with his body and his relations with the environment. In fact, we cannot specify a sharp boundary line between the body and its environment. When does a piece of meat cease being a part of the environment and become a part of the body? When it is swallowed? When it is digested? Or only later? Further, the relations of a person to parts of the environment are sometimes more intimate than his relations to parts of his own body. My personhood is often more shaped by the words I am hearing than by the skin on my left heel. In sexual intercourse a person's dependence on and intimacy with another body and another person is greater than his dependence on and intimacy with the marrow in his own bones or the hair on his own head.

We should thus be warned against isolating the individual body as if it first existed and then interacted with other things. It is itself a complex web of interactions which are interacting with the environment. Both person and body are interdependent with the environment. But the person is distinct from the environment too. Interdependence is not the same as identity.

To know myself as within nature is to know that the ecological system of interpenetration and interdependence includes me, both my body and my personality. It is not to cease to think of myself as an individual person, but it is to cease to think of a person as existing prior to or independently of his relations. These relations extend throughout the body and throughout the wider environment.

Discussion Questions

1. Is man outside nature and in opposition to it (exclusionism), or is he within it and part of it (inclusionism)? What practical consequences follow your answer?

2. Is the basis of Christian brotherly love the fact that the loved one is a real subject of feeling and action, or is it that he shares a similar relationship to God as Father? Explain.

3. How are persons related to their bodies? How does the answer to this question affect man's attitude toward the environment and toward himself?

I I

Is the Subhuman World Real?

In the first eight chapters, we saw that we need a new attitude of love and concern for the subhuman world. We can develop this new attitude only as a new vision emerges. In Chapters 9 and 10 some elements of that new vision have been sketched. Instead of viewing nature as a changeless and inexhaustible context for human action, we see all life as a fragile achievement of evolutionary processes that can be readily upset by human interference. Instead of viewing man as standing outside of nature, we see him as an interconnected part of the natural system of interdependence.

These changes in vision help to reorient us in our attitude. But this reorientation faces a very fundamental obstacle to which we have not yet attended. In our dominant Western vision the subhuman world often lacks reality in itself. Even when it is granted some reality, that reality is not the kind that would justify our love for it.

We have already considered how the biblical-Christian tradition has led to a depreciation of the subhuman world. But the point we are now considering goes much further than that. Not only is the intrinsic *value* of the subhuman world undercut, even its *reality* is questioned. At this point we have moved from theology to philosophy. The philosophical challenge to the inherent reality of the subhuman world is certainly influenced by the theological challenge to its intrinsic value. But it is more radical. Unless we can believe in the world's reality, the question of its value cannot arise.

In order to consider this new matter, we have to think about what it means for something to be real. That is a very abstract or theoretical question. It is also very important, for our unconscious philosophical assumptions have a decisive bearing on our judgments and actions. But it is not easy to become conscious of these assumptions or even to understand what is being said about them.

Let us review briefly the oft-told story of modern Western philosophy from the point of view of the reality of the subhuman world. No details are necessary. We begin, as is customary, with Descartes, who divided the world into minds and physical things. In so doing, he made a radical dualism of distinctions that had been present in both the Greek and the Christian traditions. He thereby forced a decision with respect to the status of animals, and he unhesitatingly placed them on the side of physical things. He attributed to them no feeling, no sensation, in short no subjectivity. They are to be viewed as machines, mere *its*.

Obviously, Descartes was influenced by aspects of his Christian heritage. Nevertheless, he was not merely reflecting the thought of his day. Instead, he was transforming it and thereby shaping the categories of the modern world. It is surely not without significance that the father of modern philosophy began by separating man metaphysically from all else in a way more drastic than had ever been done before in Western philosophy. In the process, he reduced everything else, the animate and the inanimate alike, to the status of mere bodies, whose major characteristic is that they are extended in space.

Descartes did at least allow the nonhuman world

the status of *being*. Its substantiality seemed to him to
reside in itself, independent of human observation.
But as modern philosophy advanced, even the objective reality of the nonhuman came under searching
questioning. The standpoint of inquiry was epistemo-
logical; that is, one asked what and how man can
know. The inquiry began with human experience and
resulted in equating reality with what men can experience or know. Approached in this way, the physical
things of Descartes became sense data for subsequent
philosophers. As sense data, they could no longer exist
in themselves as substances. Since, nevertheless, sense
data appear to the human mind as something *given,*
Berkeley taught that an active mind other than the
human must be their source. But if this is so, then
trees and dogs do not exist as objects which can be ap-
propriately loved. They are only the impressions that
God's mind works on ours.

Berkeley attributed to God the power of presenting an ordered world of sense data to man. Kant attributed this power to the human mind. In his
thought the movement toward a completely man-centered view of reality thus takes yet one step more. He
did not mean that we individually and voluntarily decide what order to project upon our environment.
The order is settled by the structure of mind itself.
This structure can be discovered by analyzing the projected order. Still "mind" means human mind, and
that mind is almost entirely alone with itself. True,
Kant allowed that there are in the environment other
entities, which he called "noumena." But these entities
are wholly outside time and space, and they have no
causal relations with anything. Since nothing can be
known or asserted of them, Kant's successors rejected
them. It is also true that Kant retained faith in God
as mind. But Kant's God was irrelevant to our experience of our environment, and with him, too, Kant's
successors dispensed.

Kant's influence upon subsequent philosophy can hardly be exaggerated. Not only Hegel and German idealism, but also more recent philosophies, such as phenomenology and existentialism, share explicitly or implicitly the vision of the human mind alone with itself. They conceive this mind in highly diverse ways. Whereas for Kant it is static, Hegel sees it as developing through history. Whereas Kant attends to the structuring activity of mind, Husserl attends to the objects of mind. But for him, too, these objects remain the objects of *mind* and not objects as they might or might not exist in themselves apart from mind. Such "things-in-themselves" he brackets out of his philosophy. The existentialists go beyond Husserl in their understanding of human existence, but they have nothing to add with respect to how other things are in themselves.

Not all recent philosophy is Kantian. Most British philosophy went on its way little affected by Kant. Since it emphasized the sense data, it is usually called "empirical." It did not acknowledge so dominant a role for mind and tried to remain closer to the scientific study of the natural world. Yet, rather than providing a more helpful vision, its results are still more pernicious with respect to our need. The Kantians have at least maintained a sense of the reality and importance of the human mind, thus providing the ground for the concern of human beings for each other. But the great empiricist Hume undermined the substantial reality of the mind as well. Although he is not entirely consistent, the implications of his thought leave us with a flux of sensuous forms and concepts devoid of being and value. Instead of lifting the nonhuman world into participation in the value of the human world, this empiricism dissolves the human one as well. The later result is a positivism in which all consideration of value is meaningless.

Against this background the ordinary language

analysis that is now dominant in the English-speaking
world is a relief. It is largely in the empirical tradition, but the paradoxical results of empiricism have
lost their hold. Since the common language corre-
sponds roughly with Aristotelian philosophy, the results of its analysis tend to return to that philosophic
tradition. On the other hand, not surprisingly, the results of ordinary language analysis tend to be determined by the common sense of the culture whose language is analyzed. In this case, it is shaped chiefly by a
post-Christian humanism. When ordinary language is
the norm, many of the philosophical obstacles to the
appropriation of the vision of the world as real and
valuable are weakened. But ordinary language philosophy cannot itself produce the new vision we need.

Thomas Aquinas received from Aristotle a philosophy that accepted the full and independent reality of
the subhuman world. He developed this doctrine into
a balanced account of the relation of man to the rest
of nature, both in his resemblance and in his difference. His influence continued through the modern period in Roman Catholic circles. In a movement called
Neo-Thomism, Thomas' realistic view vigorously entered the wider intellectual discussion. However,
through its participation in that discussion Neo-Thomism has come to stress the creativity of the human
mind in its perception of the subhuman world and to
depreciate the autonomous reality of that world—the
things in themselves. Through this recent "transcen-
dental" turn, much of contemporary Thomism has
been assimilated into the idealist tradition.

One might suppose that the natural scientists
would resist the dissolution of nature into human experience. Most of them share the naive belief that
what they investigate is more independent of their
knowledge than the dominant philosophic interpreta-
tion allows. Nevertheless, they have also contributed to

the dissolution of nature's reality. Especially in the most advanced scientific disciplines, scientists deal with a body of interrelated laws that are mathematically formulated. The question of the reality of the world to which the laws apply does not arise. The theories *seem* to describe a world that exists objectively and independently. But sophisticated philosophical interpretations of these theories often deny what on the surface they seem to say.

In addition to idealism and empiricism there is also a widespread materialism. This receives its most influential expression in Marxism, which against all the arguments of idealism and empiricism insists upon the objective and primary reality of the physical world. But that reality is named "matter," and Marxists do not see matter as an object of concern in itself. Its value is economic, and economic value is determined entirely by man's needs and desires.

Non-Marxist forms of materialism usually ally themselves closely with the technological attitude. Whatever they mean by matter, they do not attribute to it any intrinsic value. The doctrine that all things are material is used more to disparage man's claim to intrinsic value than to extend that value to other living things. What is material is there to be used and manipulated, not to be cherished and revered.

The conclusion of this survey of the major schools of modern philosophy is that none of them have attributed significant reality to things in themselves. Some have thought of the subhuman world as having some sort of purely physical, merely material, or wholly unknowable existence in itself. Others have denied even this. In either case, love or concern for man's fellow creatures would be viewed as mere sentimentality.

For most purposes it would be necessary to stress the great differences among such philosophical traditions as idealism, empiricism, and materialism. But in this chapter and those that follow, it is their agreement that is important. They all deny significant reality to the subhuman world. Where this one issue alone is in view, it will be convenient to refer to them jointly as "the dominant philosophy."

This terminology reminds us immediately that there are other strands in modern philosophy that have not acquiesced in so man-centered a view. In addition to the influence of Aristotelian, Thomistic, and common sense realism, there have been such diverse philosophies as those of Leibniz and Jonathan Edwards. Some forms of romanticism have stressed the reality and value of all of nature. The rise of the evolutionary perspective in the nineteenth century encouraged new forms of naturalism, of which Bergson's thought is influentially representative. The naturalistic tradition in America partly avoids the dominant anthropocentrism. Heidegger has devoted his philosophical career to the reopening of the question of being. Teilhard de Chardin and Alfred North Whitehead will be discussed in the chapters that follow as recent spokesmen of this subdominant tradition which does attribute reality and value to the subhuman world.

The isolation of man that is implied by the dominant philosophy has deeply affected the modern sensibility. Heidegger describes the experience of man as thrown into the world rather than as at home within it. Sartre writes of nausea. For a century alienation in its many forms has been a major motif of modern literature, and the alienation of man from his natural environment is basic to much of this experience.

But we may still ask how important is it to the man in the street that the dominant philosophy has denied significant reality to the subhuman world. He has not studied philosophy, or at least not in such a way as to be much affected by it directly. He thinks quite naively of the reality of the objects he encounters. Can we not simply bypass the philosophical discussion and call on him to accept the significant reality and intrinsic value of the subhuman world and to extend concern to it?

The answer is that indirectly, but pervasively, we are shaped by philosophy. Indeed, impressive testimony to the power of philosophical ideas over ordinary thinking is found in the writings of those most concerned about defending man's environment from further ravages. One senses in these writings a deep feeling for the goodness of a world man has not altered, for the rights of animals to have the chance to survive, for the evil of inflicting unnecessary suffering upon them. But when one studies their arguments, one finds nothing said of all this. Apparently the defenders of the subhuman world are not free to give conceptual expression to their real feelings and convictions. Marsh says of himself that as a boy, "The bubbling brook, the trees, the flowers, the wild animals were to me persons, not things." [1] This certainly cannot be considered irrelevant to his lifelong concern for the preservation and improvement of the good earth, or to his deep sensitivity to the interconnectedness of living things that enabled him to see so much that others overlooked. But his arguments for conservation are based on its importance *for man*.

The same is true of nature's defenders today. They argue that wilderness should be protected because of what it does *for man*. Man needs to be able occasionally to escape the noise, confusion, and artificiality of civilization and renew himself in a world he never made. The preservation of animal species is justified on the ground that man may yet learn new se-

1. George Perkins Marsh, quoted in Udall, *op. cit.*, p. 71.

crets from them that will benefit him. He may learn
how to avoid arthritis from the now-threatened wolverine, since almost alone among animals, the wolverine
is free from this disease. Cruelty to animals is undesirable because it breeds bad habits. Those who begin by
being cruel to animals, end by being cruel to men as
well.

Why the deep hesitation to affirm that there is
value in wilderness in itself, that biological species are
inherently worth preserving, and that individual animals have a right to happiness? The answer lies in
part in the Christian centering of all intrinsic value in
man. But it lies also in the philosophical denial of significant reality to things in themselves. The Christian
tradition cannot transform itself by the extension of
concern to man's fellow creatures without first overcoming the extreme man-centeredness of the dominant
philosophy.

Discussion Questions

1. In what senses is the subhuman world truly
    real? Explain.
2. Does whatever reality the subhuman world
    has justify a genuine human love for it?
3. Why are philosophical assumptions important
    in the conduct of human affairs? What philos-
    ophies have shaped the course of world his-
    tory in the twentieth century?
4. Are the consequences of our actions toward
    other living things important if we judge that
    they are useful for man?

12

The Philosophical Problem

None of the dominant forms of Western philosophy attribute significant reality to things in themselves. But Christian love is love for the other as it is in itself. It is not based on how the other appears or functions, how it helps or harms the lover, or how it contributes to the general good. If we are to extend Christian love beyond the human circle, we must challenge the dominant philosophy and break the hold it has upon common sense. That is a large task.

To challenge the dominant philosophy we must first understand more clearly why it takes the position it does. A simple example will help. I see a chair. I can also feel it support me. I can handle it. I affirm that it exists. But when I say that the chair exists, what am I really saying? Am I speaking of something that I can not see or feel, some thing-in-itself outside of my experience and in principle not subject to being experienced? The dominant philosophy denies that I can mean anything of this sort. By the chair, I mean just what I have experienced and can experience again. I mean the chair that is in my experience, as it is or may be in my experience. All that I mean by the chair is thus the chair *for me* or the chair *for people in general*.

It is recognized that the man in the street tends to think in naively realistic terms. He tends to think of the reality of the things he experiences as being independent of his experience. They are there, and then he happens to experience them. Some philosophers have agreed with this. But so far as they belong to the dominant school, they have noted that when we have said the object is there whether it is experienced or not, that it is there as a thing-in-itself, we have said all that can be said or thought about it. Everything else we say expresses how the object appears *to us*. Even to say that "something is there" is full of difficulties. It is hard to know what we mean in that apparently simple sentence by "something," by "is," and by "there." It is hard to think of any connection between this thing-in-itself and the thing-for-us.

One connection that seems plausible at first sight is the connection of cause and effect. We might think that the chair in itself *causes* my experience of it. But this idea, too, raises many difficulties and is generally rejected. Let us see why.

The dominant philosophy assumes that sense perception is the fundamental way in which we are related to the world. It is the starting point and basis for all our knowledge of the world. If there are other feelings, such as feelings of what is going on inside our bodies, these are to be understood as like our sensations of what is going on outside. Seeing something is the usual instance of experience that is analyzed in philosophy, and hearing and touching and tasting are assumed to be very much the same.

If experience is basically sense perception, then its objects can only be the peculiar and appropriate objects of sense perception—sense data, or perceived objects. Seeing gives us visual objects. Some think of these as patches of color. Others stress that they are colored *things,* but they do not mean colored things-in-themselves. A thing-in-itself could not be colored, since what we mean by color depends on its being seen. No matter how we come at the chair, all that we can experience of it are sense data.

Sense data can be the basis of making predictions. If I have the visual experience that I call seeing a chair, I anticipate that if I move closer and put out my hand, I will also have the tactile sensations I call touching the chair; and if I sit down, I expect to be supported. The chair is not identified with any one of these experiences. Rather what we mean by the chair has to do with all of them and with an indefinite number of other possible experiences. Again we come easily upon the idea that the unity underlying all of these varied experiences is the chair-in-itself, that the chair-in-itself is their cause.

But what do we mean here by "cause"? That is a much more difficult idea than is usually supposed. We need to take an example, and for the dominant philosophy, the standard examples come from the physical sciences and from ordinary language about the physical world. The following is a good example: Heat causes water to expand. Our question is whether the relation of the chair-in-itself to the chair-for-us can be conceived as being like the relation of heat and the expansion of water. To decide that, we have to become very clear as to what we mean by heat's *causing* the expansion of water.

First let us note what it does *not* mean. It does not mean that heat is some kind of an agent, like a man, which makes the water do something. No, what heat means here is the increase of temperature. The increase of temperature is measured by certain instruments, such as thermometers. To say that heat causes water to expand is to say that when the readings on the thermometers go up, we can observe that the volume of water also increases. Now we are back in the sphere of sense perception. We are speaking of a correlation between meter readings and other observable phenomena. Where causal relations can be affirmed.

But if cause-and-effect is a relation between observable phenomena, then it is very different from the supposed relation between the unobserved and unobservable chair-in-itself and the chair-for-us. That relation remains just as unknowable and as unthinkable as the chair-in-itself. So once again we seem to have a good reason for forgetting all about things-in-themselves. They are entirely useless for the explanation of experience, and we have no reason to talk about them at all except for experience. There is human experience and there is the world as man experiences it. About the world as it is in itself, there is nothing to be said.

I have given a very simple model of the dominant philosophy. What I have said is widely accepted in general, although each philosopher would want to restate it to bring out the proper nuance as he sees it. This matter of nuance is very important and leads to great differences among philosophers on many subjects. For the most part, however, it does not lead to a reopening of the question about whether we can have more knowledge about things-in-themselves. It is this widespread negative agreement that I have been trying to bring out.

Up to this point in this chapter, we have been trying to understand the dominant philosophy. It holds that experience is basically sense perception. Accordingly, the nonhuman world is the world known in sense perception—that is, a world of sense data. Sense data have no significant reality apart from being perceived. Given this starting point, the only role that things-in-themselves could play would be as causes of human experience of the sense data. But that does not work either. When we begin with sense perception we can only understand cause and effect as a relation be-

tween sense data. There is no way of moving from
sense perception to significant things-in-themselves.

The dominant philosophy leads to some paradoxical consequences that it usually fails to acknowledge.
These can be vividly seen in terms of the evolutionary
view of man's rise. This view is scientifically well established and almost never questioned by philosophers. But man's development out of lower forms of
life is difficult for the dominant philosophy to incor-
porate. For strict consistency this philosophy would
have to assert one of two things. Either the whole of
reality came into being abruptly out of nothing with
the advent of man; or a totally unknowable and insig-
nificant reality was transformed radically into a
human one at this point.

It will be sufficient to explain the first of these al-
ternatives. According to the dominant philosophy the
only reality of which we can usefully speak is human
experience and its perceived objects. We cannot speak
of what these perceived objects are in themselves.
Hence, before man appeared there was no reality of
which we can speak. Only when human experience
began could there be the objects of human experience
—sun and moon, wolves and cattle, sticks and stones
—whether these are conceived as sense data or as perceived objects.

This is obviously a very strange doctrine. It would
mean that all the events that produced the planet and
started the evolutionary development that culminated
in man became real abruptly, either when man
emerged or when man first learned about them. But
the whole thrust of evolutionary theory is just the op-
posite. It teaches that there were billions of years of
real occurrences, that man appeared very late, and
that no sharp line separated him from his animal
ancestors. Surely our philosophy should take account

of this scientific view of man's place in the world!

Few philosophers of the dominant tradition intend these paradoxical consequences of their man-centered view of reality. Hence, when pressed, they will
make concessions. For example, they will sometimes
acknowledge that the higher animals have experiences
too. They may even extend experience to all animals
equipped with sense organs.

But the problems of the dominant philosophy
cannot be solved by concessions. We are no better off
if we think of reality as coming into being abruptly
out of nothing with the advent of the first organ of vision, or hearing, or touch. According to all the evidence, the sense organs, too, developed gradually at
the end of a long evolutionary process.

For philosophy to take serious account of evolution would require it to transform itself radically. It
must find a way of attributing to the world out of
which animal and human experience arose a reality
that is continuous with that of human experience.
That is not easy to do. It is impossible as long as
human experience is understood basically as sense perception. Obviously there was nothing like sense perception until there was something like sense organs.

In recent times Teilhard de Chardin has provided
an influential expression of evolutionary philosophy.
He has helped us to think of experience as consciousness, or as the "within" of things. He taught that all
things have both this "within" as well as the "without"
that the dominant philosophy has had in view.

We can think of the "within" of things as what
things are in themselves. We can then understand that
the only way in which things can be viewed as having
significant reality *in* themselves is to see them as having reality also *for* themselves.

This point is crucial. The dominant philosophy
has been undecided as to whether to allow that subhu-

man things have some reality in themselves. But it has consistently assumed that if they have such reality, it is of no significance. That is because the idea of something in itself, apart from any experience whatever, really is an empty idea. If we are to attribute significant reality to something apart from our experience, it must be in terms of some other experience. When we deal with other human beings, we assume that they continue to have their experiences even when we do not experience them. They are seeing trees and buildings and other people even when we do not see them. That is why their reality and value do not depend on their reality and value for us. They exist *in* themselves as something *for* themselves. But the dominant philosophy has been reluctant to admit that nonhuman things are something *for* themselves as well.

An evolutionary philosophy must affirm that what existed before man, and before the sensory experience of animals, was already something for itself. The emergence of man and the much earlier emergence of sensory experience can still be regarded as very important events. But they can then be viewed as parts of a continuous development rather than abrupt creations out of nothing.

The acknowledgment of the reality of subhuman things for themselves cannot be treated as a minor concession within the dominant philosophy. Its implications contradict the fundamental assumptions of that philosophy. The nature of experience, of relatedness, of subject and object, and of cause and effect must all be fundamentally reconceived.

Teilhard pointed toward the philosophical reconstruction that is needed, but he did not carry it through. Fortunately, this has been done by Alfred North Whitehead. Whitehead developed his philosophy not with evolutionary problems alone in view, but in close relation also to quantum mechanics and relativity theory, as well as to theoretical issues in twentieth-century logic and mathematics. The resulting vision is the one we need. But it is not easy to understand or appropriate. The next chapter offers an introduction.

Discussion Questions

1. Can we really know things as they are in themselves? How?
2. What are some of the weaknesses of the dominant philosophy?
3. What is the difference between a thing's being real *in* itself and its being real *for* itself?

13

Whitehead: An Ecological Philosophy

In philosophy a great deal depends on the examples used. In explaining the dominant philosophy I used "seeing-a-chair" as the instance of experience to be analyzed. The dominant philosophy takes that kind of experience as basic. It understands other forms of experience, such as awareness of the functioning of one's body, experience of other people, thinking, emotional feeling, memory, and anticipation, as either analogous to the seeing of a chair or as analyzable into elements that are like it. We have already followed the inevitable consequences of this starting point.

In the previous chapter we noted that if we are to make any sense of evolution we must understand experience in some other way. Conscious sense perception must be seen to have developed gradually out of some more primitive form of experience. Whitehead points out that we know physiologically, too, that conscious sense perception is the product of complex events. There is no reason to suppose that it is a simple and primary form of experience, or that all other aspects of experience must be explained by it. We are well advised to seek more fundamental aspects of experience even if they are outside of clear consciousness.

Instead of analyzing seeing-a-chair, let us consider experiencing-in-the-present-moment-the-feeling-of-pleasure-one-had-a-moment-ago. Usually this is felt as simply continuing to enjoy that pleasure. But it is not as simple as that. Continuation through time requires renewal in each moment. And sometimes experience of the past feeling is not simply its continuation. For example, I might now feel ashamed at having felt pleasure in someone else's misfortune.

The dominant philosophy, if it would pay attention to this kind of example at all, would try to explain it on the analogy of sense perception. Sense perception does not relate us to its object as something for itself. Hence, the dominant philosophy would analyze this feeling of a past feeling as if the past feeling were a mere object for the new subject. It views the past feeling as analogous to a visual object.

Whitehead, however, turns the tables. For him, the feeling of feeling is primary. He explains in detail how clear and distinct conscious sense perceptions arise out of myriads of these far more elementary experiences. For example, the transmission of nerve impulses from cell to cell, which makes possible visual and auditory perceptions of the external world, can be analyzed into unconscious feelings of the feelings in the eye and ear and through the nerves. The final unification and projection of visual and auditory data is based on a unified human feeling of the many feelings of the cells in the brain. In the higher phases of this synthesis consciousness emerges.

The problem with the dominant philosophy is much like that with Newtonian science, which is not surprising since the two developed together. The dominant philosophy tries to understand all experience as being like ordinary sense perception. The Newtonian science tried to understand all objects as being like the objects of ordinary sense perception. Newtonian science broke down when it became clear that the ingredients which made up objects like chairs were not at all like little bits of cloth or wood, but were instead events or processes. Scientists went on to the study of electromagnetic events. But philosophers of the dominant school continued to think about the kind of reality possessed by chairs. Since it is quite implausible to think of a chair as something for itself, they quite properly continued to deny that any significant reality could be attributed to it in itself.

If, however, we turn our attention away from chairs to the electromagnetic events that make them up, the situation changes. Most of what we mean by a chair has no reality apart from its perception and use by man. Electromagnetic events were occurring for a long time before there were men, or even animals, around. They must have had their reality in themselves, and that makes sense only if we also affirm that they had reality for themselves. To have reality for itself an entity must feel. Since feeling is the most primitive form of "taking account of," and since there is excellent evidence that electromagnetic events do take account of their environment, it is reasonable to affirm that they are instances of unconscious feeling.

It is useful to recognize that reality, value, and kinship extend in this tenuous way to the most elementary particles that make up our world, but our major concern is with living things. No sharp line divides the animate from the inanimate. The features we associate with life came into being gradually at the end of a long development. Our concern for the animate must shade off into concern for the total process and the whole of reality. But it is the animate, and especially the higher forms of life, that are now threatened with extinction. It is toward these that we need to extend our sense of kinship and concern. We are fellow creatures of an age-long creative process, sharing a common history and perhaps a common destiny.

Whitehead explains that an event is alive to the extent that it includes novelty. All events repeat elements from their past. But in some events new elements appear, elements added in the event itself. This novelty may be trivial or important. The event may be more or less alive.

The things we ordinarily call alive are not individual events but vast societies of events, such as a mouse or a tree. These societies are alive to whatever extent there are events among their members whose lives affect the social organization as a whole.

Along with the novel response goes a heightening of feeling. A living event takes account of much more of its world, with far greater intensity, than does an inorganic event. The inorganic event achieves its unity by simple repetition of simple feelings. That requires the screening out of most of the complexity and intensity of feelings offered it by its world. A living event can take account of much more of its world because it achieves its unity by its own creative response. It is this greater richness of feeling and the ever new potentialities of living processes that can elicit our proper reverence.

Whitehead's philosophy pictures for us a world filled with real events, each having its own intrinsic value. Especially those that are alive significantly share with man in feeling and activity. It is therein that the needed attitude of love, concern, or reverence for living things is adequately and rationally grounded.

This philosophy also describes these real and valuable events as interrelated and interconnected in just the way that is implied by the ecological attitude. We ignore this at our peril. As Whitehead says in *Science and the Modern World,* "The two evils are: one, the ignoration of the true relation of each organism and the environment; and the other, the habit of ignoring the intrinsic worth of the environment which must be allowed its weight in any consideration of final ends." [1]

The environment of which Whitehead speaks is composed not of substances but of events. These do not first exist and then have things happen to them. They come into being only in the process of taking account of other events.

Consider, again, a moment of human experience as an event. That momentary experience comes into being and then passes away. It grows out of the preceding moment of human experience. It also takes account of what is going on in the body and in the wider environment. It does not first exist as something else and then take account of these things. It comes into being as a process of taking account of these other events. Without them it would not be what it is. They give it its content.

What is true of a human experience is true of all events. Each comes into being as a process of taking account of other events. It has no other being or reality. It is not identical with the events it feels. Its reality for itself is unique and irreducible. But it is not independent. It exists only as a synthesis of its world.

Just as each event comes into being as a taking account of its world, so every event becomes a part of the world of which subsequent events must take account. The consequences of each event spread out in complex ways through the entire future, interacting with the consequences of all the other events. The whole universe is one vast ecological system. Both the events that make up the human personality and those that constitute the cells in the human body belong to that system.

There is still another way in which the environ-

1. (New York: The Macmillan Co., 1925; New York: New American Library, Mentor Books, 1948, p. 175.)

ment enters into a man and constitutes him. Seeing a landscape or a painting is not an incidental occurrence that leaves a man fundamentally unaffected. On the contrary, the beauty of nature or art shares in constituting his very being. Whitehead shows us that the beauty of the environment "adds to the permanent richness of the soul's self-attainment." [2]

It is clear that the ordinary ways of separating history from nature, or man from his fellow creatures, are undercut in Whitehead's vision. In conclusion, it will be useful to note one final way in which Whitehead frees us from this dualism.

In the Newtonian age men were impressed by natural law as something immutably binding physical things. In man they found a freedom that transcended such law. This freedom, they thought, distinguished man and the history he makes from law-bound nature.

In this respect, too, the Newtonian vision has broken down in science, but it retains considerable power in philosophy and in the general vision of reality out of which men operate. However, in Whitehead's view, even the laws of nature are not immutable. There are innumerable events each taking account of its world in its own way. The individual events constitute themselves in some measure unpredictably, but for the most part they reenact dominant elements in their past. When we are dealing with vast numbers of them, and in the physical sciences we usually are, the indeterminateness of the behavior of each individual is unimportant. The behavior of the aggregate can be predicted within narrow limits and with high probability. We can formulate these predictive descriptions in "laws." But if so, then laws are a function of the behavior of real things in the world. They do not deter-

2. *Op. cit.*, p. 180.

mine that behavior. The behavior determines them and the behavior can change. With the emergence of new societies new laws emerge.

The emergence of new laws is most apparent in the historical process. The laws describing the average behavior of contemporary Americans in sexual relations did not exist before contemporary Americans existed. They will change gradually as the behavior of individual Americans changes. Most of the laws of the social sciences are of this sort.

Laws about the behavior of biological species are similar. These laws come into being with the evolutionary emergence of the species, change with its evolutionary development, and cease to operate if the species is exterminated. The laws about homing pigeons depend upon the behavior of individual homing pigeons. If new behavior patterns are developed by breeding, the laws will change.

Of course, human beings differ from each other much more than animals of a single species differ. Human culture changes much more rapidly than animal behavior patterns. The difference is very great and very important. These and other differences can and should be described in detail. This description can be carried through in the categories of Whitehead's philosophy. The differences should be stressed and affirmed as the objective justification for man's peculiar concentration of concern on his own survival and welfare. But they are differences within a single world, whether we call it nature, or history, or an ecological system. They do not make man an outsider. They do not reduce the other products of the creative evolutionary process to mere objects without intrinsic value. There is no dualism of man and his environment.

Discussion Questions

1. What is meant by saying that electromagnetic events are "instances of unconscious feeling"? Does this give them "value"? How does this justify extending love, concern, and reverence to the subhuman world?
2. Are events really as interrelated as Whitehead says they are?
3. Does "natural law" have the same meaning when applied both to man and to the subhuman world? Explain.

14

The Commitment We Need

For traditional Christianity, the transcendent creator alone is sacred. Man and the rest of the world are jointly God's creation. As created they have value derived from their creator. From this agreed point, there can be two lines of development. It is possible, on the one side, to stress that all God's creatures are valuable to God and, hence, in themselves. In this case it is natural and proper to emphasize man's cocreaturehood with all and to extend love to all. But on the other side, Christianity teaches that man alone is made in the image of God and that God has established him as lord over all other creatures. It sometimes so accentuates man's supreme and unique importance that all other things become mere means to his ends. This tendency has dominated Western Christendom. Even here, however, some sense of stewardship is encouraged. Man may be lord of all other creatures, but he is accountable to a far superior lord, the creator of all.

Traditional Christianity is still an important force, but for several centuries its influence in the West has been declining. Its major successor has been humanism. Some forms of humanism have stressed their continuity with Christianity; others have emphasized their opposition. Whether or not belief in God is retained by the humanist, he shifts the real locus of the sacred to man. In this way, the process of separating man from his fellow creatures, already begun in traditional Christianity, is completed. Other living things have no significant reality or value except in relation to man. They belong to him, and he owes no accounting to anyone except himself for how he uses them. Concern for these creatures as they are in themselves would be pure sentimentality. Animals, for example, exist for the humanist only as pets, sources of energy, livestock, game, pests, specimens, or occasionally, aesthetic objects.

Humanism is today the most unifying form of faith. Traditional religions tend to emphasize their humanistic elements in order to be relevant in our time. Humanism is expressed in the charter of the United Nations and guides the more enlightened leaders in the developing nations. But, like traditional Christianity, humanism is declining. The reason for the decline has little to do with its attitude toward animals. The reason is its inherent instability.

Humanism thrives on attacking otherworldly and superstitious elements in traditional religion and culture. Against them it calls for the affirmation of present human values and the application of critical reason to the solution of man's problems. But it has no new basis or ground for its affirmation of man. It derives its vision of the sacredness of human personality from the traditional Christianity it rejects.

Indeed, it is difficult for humanism to state clearly where its commitment lies. Is there a sacred essence of humanity in which all men participate? Or is the object of commitment the sum total of all individual human beings now alive? Is it human personality as it actually exists that is sacred? Or are we to commit ourselves to the realization of a potential that has not yet been actualized?

Important practical consequences follow from the

answers to these questions. Some answers indicate that the unlimited multiplication of human life is desirable, regardless of the problems which that creates. Other answers indicate that the realization of the human essence or potential is far more important than the multiplication of individuals. But no matter how the questions are answered, serious difficulties arise. The critical rationality that humanists have directed against traditional religions plays havoc with humanism as well. Its arbitrary elements become more and more apparent, and as this occurs, its power to elicit commitment declines.

The operation of critical reason on humanist pretensions leads to secular atheism. For secular atheism nothing is sacred, or ultimate, or absolute. Hence, there are no *basic* commitments, only provisional ones. Everything is seen as means to ends which are themselves judged by their contributions to further ends. All belief in the sacred is perceived as a threat to the needed pragmatic rationality. The strong man can recognize the relativity of all values. He does not need to believe that actions have *ultimate* importance in order to take them. He can establish his own norms and live effectively by them without the illusion that they have a higher sanction. Indeed, by removing all such sanctions, he believes that he can have greater freedom and greater tolerance of the freedom of others. Even if there is some pain in the loss of the sacred, he prefers to live freely and without illusion rather than to submit again to authority.

Secular atheism has two conflicting tendencies in relation to the subhuman world. On the one hand, since it denies the sacredness of human personality, it deflates human pretensions to distinctiveness and thinks of man as much more like the other animals. On the other hand, it subscribes to the thoroughly man-centered philosophies of empiricism and positivism. Furthermore, the recognition of kinship between man and the other animals tends rather to disparage the worth of man as an object of concern than to encourage concern for other living things. Secular atheism is closely associated with the technological attitude and tends to apply it even to the treatment of men.

Humanism gains its power by freeing man from the shackles of superstition and displays its weakness when required to stand on its own feet. Similarly, secular atheism gains its power by its clear-sighted critique of both traditional religion and humanism and finds that it has little to offer in itself. On many university campuses it no longer plays the role of rebel; for it is now established as academic orthodoxy. At this point its barrenness and emptiness become apparent. It has little to say on the important issues of life. It hides its nakedness in specializations of questionable usefulness. It claims freedom from all absolutes, but it has no ends toward which to use its freedom. It turns away from the interior life and treats all things, including men, as objects. The objectivity it achieves belongs to death rather than life.

At least these are the criticisms directed against secular atheism by many of the youth who come into contact with it. Largely in reaction to it, there is arising now a fresh and vital paganism. Men are rediscovering the sacred in the dance, in communal intimacy, and in the mysteries of bodily feeling. The popular musical *Hair* celebrates this new tribalism with evangelical fervor. The new pagans are irreverent toward the traditional Christian and humanistic symbols of the sacred. They are not concerned with displaying the sacred as either unified or transcendent. They are satisfied in the immediacy of the experience of the sacred power. They call on us to regain the lost awareness of the sacred in all the varied experiences of life. Then we will stop treating these experiences as prag-

matic means to some future or transcendent good and
enjoy them as ends in themselves. Not theories about
the universe, but the concentration of energy and feeling in the now is the proper expression of this renewal of religious experience.

In general the new paganism, like the old, is far
more in tune with the vitalities and rhythms of nature
than are traditional Christianity, humanism, and secular atheism. The sacred is found not only in human
community and bodily ecstasy but in the natural environment as well. The healing of man and society is regarded as requiring a new balance and harmony with
the subhuman world. Men must find themselves in
and with the natural processes rather than outside and
against them. Those human feelings that rise directly
out of the organism are trusted more than those that
have been culturally molded.

The new paganism has a much more affirmative
message than the atheistic secularism with which it
vies on the university scene. But it, too, has its weaknesses. It, too, is more powerful in its protest against
the aridity of the dominant atheism than in its own
independent affirmations. The secular atheist rightly
points out that these affirmations cannot be taken
quite seriously in the adult world. The critical faculty
is too well established in our culture. It can be set
aside for short periods of recreation or celebration,
but we cannot ignore the fact that our actions have
consequences that we need to consider before we act.
The blind quest for an immediacy in which to lose
self-awareness is humanly destructive. We should at
least use rational criteria in deciding which gods to
worship. But when we examine what the new paganism finds to be sacred, it often appears as nothing
more than certain types of experience that can be in-
duced in controlled ways. As such, they lose their sacredness and become just one more part of the secular

world. The blind quest for community is not only escapist but dangerous. Communities can be competitive and mutually destructive. When they are viewed as sacred, the possibility of criticizing their actions, and thereby gaining independence from them, is lost. A new tribalism is the last thing we need on a crowded planet. It would prove divisive rather than unifying. It can provide no responsible guidance for the vast industrial and economic changes that must occur if we are to survive the ecological crisis.

There is truth in the criticisms directed by each of these movements against the other. Thus far the degree of truth has been partly obscured by the remaining power of humanism within them. The man who thinks he rejects the sacred entirely sometimes continues to assume the peculiar importance and worth of man as man in a way his own principles do not justify. In this way he is saved from the worst consequences of his atheism. Likewise, the new paganism is still far more humanistic than the old. Thus a principle of self-criticism is present that still functions effectively from time to time. But we cannot assume that humanistic habits will last indefinitely. As they are outgrown, the inherent weaknesses of both movements will be increasingly obvious.

Neither secular atheism nor the new paganism provides the focus for a long-term commitment to the healing of our natural environment. Secular atheism is involved in technological attitude. It is suited to the efficient achievement of arbitrary ends. The ends are usually set by a society that is still largely humanistic or nationalistic. The new paganism has recovered a sense of unity with the environment and respect for it, but in the commitment to immediacy it has abandoned the critical reflection apart from which we cannot cope with our ecological problems.

We cannot return to humanism even though it

continues to be pervasively influential. Its internal instability is now too obvious. In any case, its separation of man from his world is just what we do not want. We need a new, inclusive commitment that will direct our concern to the subhuman world as well as to man and that will guide and sustain intelligent action through thick and thin.

An apparent solution would be to view all nature, or at least all life, as sacred. Thereby we would achieve the goal of inclusiveness. But in other respects this would be calamitous. There is truth, if only a very one-sided truth, in the bitter poem by Matthew Arnold ironically entitled "In Harmony with Nature."

Know, man hath all which Nature hath, but more,
And in that *more* lie all his hopes of good.
Nature is cruel, man is sick of blood;
Nature is stubborn, man would fain adore;
Nature is fickle, man hath need of rest;
Nature forgives no debt, and fears no grave;
Man would be mild, and with safe conscience blest.
Man must begin, know this, where Nature ends;
Nature and man can never be fast friends.
Fool, if thou canst not pass her, rest her slave! [1]

These lines express much that has proved destructive in Western man's vision of his relation to nature. Their spirit must be profoundly rejected if we are to respond adequately to our present crisis. But Arnold's point cannot be ignored. As Whitehead pointed out, life is robbery. Life preys on life. In the quest to sustain their own lives and to perpetuate their species, animals are ruthless in the destruction of other life, plant or animal. Man, too, must participate in this

1. In *Poetical Works of Matthew Arnold* (New York: The Macmillan Co., 1910), p. 5.

process of destruction, but he should not make it the object of his commitment.

The concern we need to extend to all things is better symbolized by stewardship than by commitment. To commit ourselves either to individual living things or to the sum total of all would inhibit responsible stewardship rather than promote it. Stewardship must be governed not only by respect for the goodness things embody but also by a vision of the good that is yet to be realized.

Yet stewardship is not an adequate concept either. Whereas it suggests that man is an outsider; instead, man is a part of that for which he is concerned and responsible. Whereas it suggests that man brings adequate knowledge with him to his task and can control what occurs; instead, he must learn from the world for which he cares how to serve and work with it.

The better image is of a participant in a process of healing and growth. Such a participant has responsibilities, but he is not the master. There is something going on that he does not manage, something that he must learn to adjust to and work with. Since he is himself part of nature, he can recognize that process working in himself, both in his body and in his personality, as well as in his environment. He can develop sensitivity to that process and by restraint and openness assist its working both within and without.

The process which we cannot manipulate, but whose working we can facilitate, must be discriminated from the totality of events in the universe. It is not expressed in hurricanes, or earthquakes, or the force of gravity, although these, too, are parts of nature. It is the process that makes for life and the enrichment of life, variety of forms, intensity of experience, consciousness, and love.

But this process is not identical with the individual things that it has produced. Toward the individual things love or concern is the attitude we need. But toward the process that gives them life and enriches life another attitude is appropriate. To it we can commit ourselves. This commitment need not be hesitant, provisional, or tentative. It can and should be basic. If this process is what we mean by "nature" or "life," then we can and should view "nature" or "life" as sacred. But it will be better to speak of it as Creative Process or as God.

To commit ourselves to God, understood in this way, would be to seek to promote life in its variety and intensity as well as in its consciousness and love. It would encourage reflective inquiry and selective appraisal of the relation of means and ends. But it would also encourage sensitivity, passion, and community. It would provide a critical norm by which to evaluate the many claimants to loyalty and service. It would undergird our commitment to a healthy balance of human and subhuman life and would keep us sensitive to the total ecological consequences of our acts. It would encourage and even require just that extension of love to the subhuman world that is the hallmark of the new Christianity.

Discussion Questions

1. What are some of the strengths and weaknesses of humanism, secular atheism, and the new paganism?
2. Should all life be considered sacred?
3. Should our basic attitude to the world be one of commitment? Of stewardship? Of healing?
4. Does the creative process have an absolute value? Does it make sense to call the process

that produces life, variety, intensity, consciousness, and love—"God"? Why is this process not expressed in hurricanes or earthquakes? Is it fair to single out the life-giving rather than death-dealing elements of the total process?

15

Is Commitment Possible?

Many will agree that to commit ourselves to the process that creates and sustains life, variety, intensity, consciousness, and love would be useful and beneficial. But is such commitment possible?

If commitment were something entirely voluntary, this question would not arise. Provisional commitments are like that. In order to work for peace, one is quite free to commit himself provisionally to campaigning for a peace candidate. He has only to choose. But here it is a matter of *basic* commitment. Our basic commitments arise in response to our sense of something that is *absolutely* important or good, something sacred. They arise as we are "grasped" by something rather than through choice.

If that were the whole story, however, there would be no point in discussing basic commitments at all. They would just happen at random. Actually the relation between choosing and being chosen is more complicated than that. Even our basic commitments are subject to erosion through critical reflection, as the histories of Christianity and humanism show. Similarly, as a new way of looking at the world arises, new features take on importance. One can train himself to view matters in a new light and even to act in new ways. Even *basic* commitments are partly shaped in this way.

Still it remains true that basic commitments emerge and are not simply chosen. It would be useless to call for a basic commitment to something whose absolute importance and goodness could not be made apparent, and thereby grasp the human spirit. Hence, one cannot sensibly call for commitment to something that on closer inspection appears unworthy or unreal.

The question must be asked here: Is the process that produces life, variety, intensity, consciousness, and love such that, as we examine it more closely, our sense of its importance and worth is enhanced? Or is the reverse the case?

Suppose that on examination we found the phrase misleading. It implies that there is some significant unity since we can talk of "*the* process." Perhaps on examination we would find that the process that produces life and the process that produces love are quite distinct and even incompatible. Then the call for commitment in its present form would be meaningless. At best, one would have to choose between the process that makes for life and the one that makes for love.

Or suppose that on examination we decided that there is no single factor or process that makes for life. Perhaps there are only myriads of blind happenings which from time to time in varied and unpredictable ways produce or sustain life. Then again the call to commitment would be meaningless.

I am convinced that examination of the process does not lead to either of these conclusions, that one and the same factor in the universe functions to produce and sustain life wherever it occurs and encourages in man the widest extension of his concern to other living beings. But all such affirmations about reality confront much doubt and incredulity. They involve beliefs about the world that do not fit comfortably with the intellectual habits of our time. For that reason, these beliefs seem implausible or irrelevant.

Further, the ordinary idea of a process or a factor in the universe is so vague, that it is useless to call for commitment to it and meaningless to call it God.

The major reason for the decline of belief in God in the modern world is that this belief has seemed increasingly out of step with the rest of modern thought. Part of the awkwardness stemmed from scientific discoveries. The ordinary presentation of belief in God implied things that did not correspond with reliable scientific theory. Certainly this weakened the credibility of theism. But this was not the basic problem. Theism could be modified, and was modified, to fit the facts as they became known. Part of the difficulty came from the authoritarian way the doctrine was presented and the authoritarian cast given to the belief itself. Certainly this alienated many of the most creative and sensitive moderns. But this was not the basic problem either. Theism could be presented in a fully liberal spirit, and it often was. The basic problem was that it could not be successfully modified to fit the vision of reality expressed in the dominant philosophy.

The dominant philosophy has declared human experience to be the measure of all things. Man is the measure not only of value or importance, but also of reality or being. Dogs and chairs have no reality except as they function in human experience. The same is true of God. From the point of view of the dominant philosophy, the reality of God can only be his reality for man.

To think of the process that produces life and has produced it through millions of years as having its reality only for man is a very confusing idea. We try to picture the process as it appears to man, and we fail. Hence, the notion of such a process cannot grasp our imagination, and the process itself cannot evoke our commitment. Unless the process is fully real in itself, and unless we can seriously think of it as such, the needed commitment cannot arise. This is the crux of the problem.

Theologians have sometimes made a virtue of this situation. We know nothing, they declare, of what God is in-and-for himself. In any case, it would be a merely conceptual knowledge, and the attempt to gain it would be an expression of lack of faith. They warn that when we try to think about God as he is in himself, we put *our* concepts in place of the living God or reduce God to a creature of our minds. According to these theolgoians, our only concern should be what God is for us. And what God is for us is what is revealed in Jesus Christ. In Christ, they say, we have saving knowledge of God, and this is the only knowledge of himself that God grants us.

Now this view, held by many of the leading Protestant theologians of the last generation, is not to be lightly dismissed. Certainly it is more important to know how God deals with us than to know something about God that is irrelevant to us. Yet the position must be rejected. It does not work. There are good logical reasons why it does not work, and the actual results in our generation have borne out these reasons. This view of the relation of God to man as given *only* in Christ has led with perfect consistency to the atheistic Christianity of our time. The leaders of that movement were brought up on the view I have been describing. It did not work for them. Let me explain.

When one said in those days that God is known only in Jesus Christ, he still assumed that the word God in that sentence meant something. He did not mean to say simply that Jesus Christ is known only in Jesus Christ. That would not have been very interesting. He meant that some kind of transcendent and even omnipotent reality made itself known in Jesus Christ. But what is presupposed in the sentence is then denied by it too. To have a notion of something transcendent and omnipotent and to bring that notion

with you to be reshaped by Jesus Christ is one thing.
To have no notion at all and to come blankly to Jesus
Christ is another. If one does the former, he does not
know God only in Jesus Christ, although in his en-
counter with Jesus he may discover how inadequate
and even false' was his earlier notion of God. If one
does the latter, he will have no more reason to speak
of God after meeting Jesus than before. In meeting
Jesus he will have met *only* Jesus. If someone tells
him that Jesus is sometimes called God, it will mean
nothing more than if some other proper name is given
him. If God is known only in Jesus Christ, then he
quite simply must be Jesus Christ, and nothing is
gained by using this additional name.

Of course no one has ever really meant that, or
more accurately, those who do mean that have stopped
talking about God. The theologians of the last generation talked a great deal about God and said many
things about him they would not have said about
Jesus. But they used this doctrine to forbid raising the
question as to what the word God means. They spoke
as if "God" pointed to some reality that was objectively real to and for man, but they turned attention
away from the question as to whether that was the
case and, if so, how it could be the case. Those were
philosophical questions, and they opposed the intru-
sion of philosophy into theology.

If we now try to speak of God, again we face the
philosophical problem behind this theological position. The dominant philosophy only allows us to
speak of God as he is for us, just as it only allows us
to speak of dogs and pencils as they are for us. The
dominant philosophy, however, introduces an additional difficulty in speaking of God. Since we can see
and touch dogs and pencils, even if they have no reality for themselves, they do have indubitable reality for
us. But God does not appear in sense experience.

That God does not appear in sense experience

has been a basic part of the whole biblical-Christian tradition. But it has not led to disbelief because it has been accompanied by two other beliefs: God is at least sometimes experienced nonsensuously; and what is experienced through the senses or otherwise gives evidence of God's reality. However, the dominant philosophy has made difficulties for both of these doctrines.

The dominant philosophy may admit that there are some nonsensuous feelings, such as the feeling of the holy, that are associated with belief in God. But such experience must be understood as analogous to sense experience. The holy we experience is nothing other than a part of our experience. Furthermore, in this perspective, whereas the pencil and dog do not belong only to my private experience but also to that of many other people, my experience of the holy is quite simply my own. Such purely private experiences are generally disparaged. And even if they are fully admitted, we are left only with a bit of private experience. To call that God would be odd indeed.

Primarily, Christians have assumed that the events of history and nature as well as private experience have given them warrant to speak of a reality that is not identical with those events. The way one reasons from what is given to something not given is by arguing from an effect to its cause. But in the dominant philosophy, one cannot reason from the world or any aspect of it to God as its cause. On its principles the cause like the effect must belong to the contents of experience. Perhaps a feeling of the holy might be the cause of worship. But in these terms God cannot be the cause of anything. If he is not the cause of anything, there is no reason to suppose that he exists or that, if he did exist, it would make any difference.

Whitehead, we saw, holds to quite different principles. Experience is basically and primarily nonsensory. It begins with the feeling of our past and of

our bodies. What is felt is experienced as having had
its own reality in and for itself. That this is so is evi-
denced in aspects of our surest and most pervasive beliefs, but it is not clearly given in vivid consciousness.
We reason from clear consciousness to what must have
been in order that this consciousness be as it is. Our
consciousness is an effect of causes.

There is no proof here of the reality of God, but
the question is entirely open. No special pleading,
leap of faith, or appeal to dogma is required. Along
with our dim but pervasive experience of our past
feelings, of our bodies, and of our environing world, is
there also an experience of a creative process? If so,
there is reason to affirm God as real in and for himself, just as the past experiences, the body, and the environing world are real in and for themselves. Whitehead believes that the order and especially the novelty
that characterize every experience, as well as the aim
of each experience to fulfill some relevant possibility,
bear witness that a creative influence is effective in
every event. He sees evidence also in the special intui-
tions and experiences of the world's great religious figures. Most followers of Whitehead have agreed that
there are reasons to speak of God.

I have been sketching how the same doctrines
that have concealed from us the autonomous reality
and value of the subhuman world also excluded the
possibility of believing in God. The same philosophical reform that opens up the possibility of affirming
unabashedly the autonomous reality of the subhuman
world also reopens the question of God. Hence the
discussion of God's reality should begin. In *this* context it makes sense.

For the discussion to begin afresh, it should be
really open not only with respect to God's reality but
also with respect to what he is like. A God who plays
a discernible role in every experience and every event

is a very different God than one likened to a watch-maker who observes the results of his handiwork from a distance. He differs also from the supernatural deity who intervenes from time to time to benefit his favor-ites. A God who is affected by all that happens, suffer-ing in all suffering and rejoicing in all rejoicing, is very different from the impassive deity of an earlier orthodoxy. And a God who always persuades and never coerces or compels is very different from the omnipotent sovereign to whose will all must resign themselves.

The difference is indeed great, so great that some have suggested that the old word God should be aban-doned if our evidence points, as Whitehead thought, to this kind of a reality. Perhaps we should speak only of Life, of Nature, or of Creative Process. Perhaps we should speak of the Word or of Christ, since the every-where active, suffering, persuading, life-giving reality who emerges from Whitehead's analysis is recognized by him as manifest in a peculiar way in Jesus.

I am not ready to make this change in terminol-ogy. It is my hope that we can rescue the word God from the oppressive and repressive and unreal conno-tations it has come to have for so many people. Per-haps we can give it new meaning, at once more Chris-tian and more universal, at once more personal and more natural. But if this is what we are to do, we must not think in terms of recovering old beliefs about God but about discovering him afresh. Of course, there will be elements of recovery. Every new growth must have its roots in the past. If there were no continuity, it would be wrong to speak of God at all. But the vision we need of nature and of man's place in it cannot develop by repeating a past view, whether biblical or traditional. It will reflect and be shaped by that history. But it must grow out of reflec-tion on ecology, evolution, human biology, and contemporary philosophy as well. Likewise, a view of God to be viable in our time must develop in intimate relation with all that we know of the universe and its total history, and of the role of man within it. It will not do to take a received idea and adapt it only under the pressure of necessity when its falsity and irrelevance are forced on our attention. Our view of God must not be a reluctant compromise with science and modernity. It must be fully rooted in our present situation, fully affirming what the evidence suggests.

I do not mean that we should believe only what a majority of the wise men of our time believe. The majority have rarely been right. In any case, when I speak of finding God afresh in our time I am speaking as a Christian. Christians are those who have been shaped in their perception of meaning and importance and in the very structure of their existence by Jesus. What we as Christians seek when we seek God in our time is not sought by all. Our questions are not the same as those that have been formed by the dominant philosophy. We are driven by concerns that do not drive all men. The God we seek is the Christian God. But what we today find as the Christian God may differ profoundly from the God of Augustine, of Thomas, of Calvin, of Schleiermacher, or of Barth.

For example, if we now use the language of creation, we will not be referring to some one act of God thousands or billions of years ago. We will not be speaking of the once-for-all ordaining of supposed immutable laws of nature. Such a view may have made sense in the Newtonian age, but it makes none in ours. It could have importance only if it were supposed that God would intervene in his creation from without to save man from the consequences of his actions. But to believe that is to undercut human responsibility and to run counter to ages of human experience and spiritual maturation.

The creative action of God which concerns us is the creation that takes place now, moment by moment, in our environment and in ourselves. In each moment God confronts the totality of the past with new possibilities. How the world responds, whether in acceptance or rejection of these possibilities, God does not determine. He creates by persuasion in and through the free decisions of his creatures. To believe in God is to trust his creative work amongst and within us, to adapt ourselves to it, to attend to it as it operates in all creatures, to sensitize ourselves to it as it works in us, and to respond to its call to new risks.

Belief in God is thus not only a part of a total vision within which science and technology can become servants of life rather than conquerors of nature. It is also the basis of the kind of response to the present crisis apart from which this crisis may be man's last.

Discussion Questions

1. Why has the dominant philosophy made it so hard for man to believe in God? Is human experience really the measure of all things?
2. Discuss: "Our only religious concern should be what God is *for us*."
3. Do we experience a creative process? Is this an experience of God?
4. How much can we change our idea of God and still be Christian?

16

Is It Too Late?

There are many consequences that follow from what has been said. Artists, writers, journalists, philosophers, and scientists need to work together with politicians, economists, technicians, and naturalists to form the new consciousness that we need and to work out its implications for personal conduct, social order, and international relations. A task of special importance and magnitude falls upon the churches. Despite their loss of power and prestige, they remain the major religious institutions of our society and the bearers of a great heritage. If the vision and life we now need is a new, more naturalistic Christianity, and not primitivism, or Taoism, or paganism, or secular humanism, then the church is particularly challenged to carry through its own transformation and to give leadership in the shaping of this new vision of reality. Vision and commitment are formed above all in worship. In the quest for new and more relevant forms of worship, the churches must take great care as to what is communicated through these new forms. They have in their hands instruments of enormous power. Let them take care how they use these instruments.

The church has another task as well—to promote the needed spirit of personal and national sacrifice for the larger and the longer good. This has been central to Christian self-understanding throughout the centuries. The cross of Jesus Christ is the focus of our faith, and we know that we are called on to take up our own crosses. In recent years the call to sacrifice has often been muted. We have heard more about self-fulfillment and self-realization than about self-denial. But the time has come to return to this more basic theme of Christian tradition. For the sake of future generations, our generation is called upon to repent of its self-indulgent ways, to discipline itself, and to accept reductions in the standard of living to which it has grown so quickly accustomed. As individuals we are called upon to give up goals we have long sought and the leisure and relaxation we so enjoy in order to take actions that antagonize our erstwhile friends.

Activists may grow impatient with all this talk. To them it seems that new knowledge and new laws —not a new vision, or consciousness, or spirit—are all we need. If we stand on the brink of catastrophe, if decisions that will be made tomorrow will settle our fate, then is not all this talk of changes in our basic attitudes, changes that will certainly require years, irrelevant and distracting? Above all, should we not give up talking about God and concentrate instead on the tasks ahead? These are serious questions, and they should be seriously regarded. Is it, perhaps, already too late?

Certainly the projection of present trends for even two or three decades is frightening. The rate of growth of world population is likely to increase. New grains will temporarily ease the problem of food shortages, but they will heighten our dependence on a few crops. Crop failures will have increasingly disastrous results over wider areas. The percentage of the world population whose brains have been permanently damaged by lack of proteins in childhood will increase. The urgency of finding new sources of food will lead to the decimation of the most edible types of ocean fish. Under the pressure to produce food, more forests will be cut down and marginal land brought under cultivation. The permanent loss of topsoils will be accelerated. Meanwhile, the use of agricultural chemicals will increase, poisoning streams and lakes and killing birds. Poisons will continue to find their way up the food chain to the human body. Wild animals above the size of small rodents will disappear outside of zoos. These rodents, like insects, will become increasingly difficult to control as their natural enemies are exterminated. We will resort to wholesale poisoning with further damage to the environment.

Pollution of the oceans will increase rapidly. Large portions will be covered by oil. The coral islands will disintegrate. The coastal areas will be poisoned, and all the varieties of marine life dependent on them will disappear. If plankton are decimated, the results will be still more horrendous, for plankton are the basis of the food chain in the ocean.

A blanket of smog will cover the planet reducing agricultural output and shortening human life. Local conditions will vary. Temporary concentrations of smog will kill thousands of people in cities, and life in some areas will depend on the use of gas masks and oxygen tanks.

Scientists disagree as to the effect that man's present style of life will have on planetary temperatures. Some anticipate a new ice age that will greatly reduce the habitable portions of the planet. Others expect a warming trend that will melt the polar ice caps. If this occurs, the level of the oceans will rise enough to submerge many of the world's greatest cities.

As habitable space declines, and as both land and sea become less productive, population *cannot* continue to expand. Unless air and water pollution and the poisoning of our bodies through food greatly shorten life expectancy, hundreds of millions of people will have to starve before a new balance is achieved between population and food supply.

This is a depressing projection, and many will regard it as unduly pessimistic. Perhaps the efforts now being made here and there to check population growth through birth control will spread and become more successful. Perhaps agricultural technology will prevent massive crop failures and further deterioration of the soil. Perhaps international treaties can control fishing in order to assure an optimum supply for future generations. Perhaps men will stop using the oceans as the depository for wastes, find ways of avoiding oil spills or of cleaning them up, and cease poisoning the coastal areas with sewage and chemicals. Perhaps worldwide efforts against air pollution will be successful, and the present planetary temperature will be maintained.

But projection of past trends does not give us much assurance along these lines. Short-term gains and local interests usually win out in competition with long-term advantages and the larger good. When immediate needs are a matter of survival itself, restraint for the sake of others is hard to foresee.

It is equally possible to argue that these projections are too optimistic. They ignore the fact that the crises in food and pollution and the exhaustion of resources come at a time when mankind is in possession of ultimate weapons. Since Hiroshima and Nagasaki we have known that the human race lives under the threat of total extinction. To our atomic arsenal we have added equally lethal chemical and bacteriological weapons. Thus far the balance of terror has worked. We survived the Cuban confrontation. We have exercised restraint in Vietnam. We may survive the still more serious crisis in the Middle East.

But as world population grows and resources decline, tensions will be heightened. The present tone of international relations will seem calm and relaxed in retrospect. In addition, more and more nations will gain possession of apocalyptic weapons. Can we expect a people facing a real threat of extinction to refrain from unleashing the ultimate weapon and allow its enemies to be victorious?

How do we react to this somber picture of our situation? I shall speak for myself in the belief that others resemble me. My first reaction is refusal of serious belief. The individual facts I may not be able to dispute, but I deny to myself that the situation is really that bad. The authorities, with all the power and knowledge at their disposal, will certainly take care of it. I shall put in my two cents' worth on this issue, as on others, to salve my conscience and to bolster my self-image as a concerned citizen, but beyond that I shall conduct business as usual, assuming that the future will be much like the past, putting out of my mind the apocalyptic threat under which we live.

However, there are times when the recognition of the planet's dying breaks through my defenses. Then my reaction tends to be one of despair. If all the present trends lead toward destruction, must I not realistically accept the early end of human life as inevitable? What use is it to attempt the impossible task of altering the course of history, especially when my influence is so slight?

It is important to recognize the great similarity of these two responses of complacency and despair. Their results are almost identical. They let *me* off the hook. I am left free to eat, drink, and be merry—or more realistically, to enjoy my family, my friends, and my work—for there is no real problem to whose solution I am called to contribute. Either others will solve it or it is insoluble. My attention can be directed toward the immediate and manageable issues of daily living.

Realistic hope represents a third alternative to

complacency and despair. The man who hopes can
view the threat unflinchingly. He does not deny its seriousness either in his thoughts or in his feelings. Yet
his hope is the refusal of despair. The man who hopes
is the man who seeks openings, assumes responsibility,
endures failure after failure, and still seeks new openings for fresh efforts.

In the depths of a depression Franklin Delano
Roosevelt once said that the only thing we had to fear
was fear itself. Today, facing the many trends that
hurl us toward the abyss, we might say analogously,
our only hope is hope itself. If we react in complacency or despair, there is no hope for human survival.
If, instead, we hope, the future lies before us, full of
uncertainties and risks, yet containing also hope.

But how can there be hope? To tell ourselves to
hope in order that there be hope is, in the long run,
futile. Hope rests on something other than its own
usefulness. A partial answer is that hope is a matter of
temperament or disposition, something to be dealt
with, if at all, by psychologists. Perhaps such a temperament is closely connected with the basic trust one de-
velops in the early months of his life when he is fortu-
nate in his maternal care.

But there are other dimensions of hope, dimensions we can call existential, or religious, or even
theological. In some measure hope is a function
of what we believe, and in this global crisis, it is a
function of what we believe *ultimately and compre-
hensively*.

The Old Testament found hope in the antici-
pated interventions of a transcendent God. The New
Testament looked forward to the apocalyptic end of
an unacceptable history. Few of us can live with these
visions of reality, and their collapse in the last three
centuries seems to have removed the grounds of hope
for many people. In much of our youth culture, hope

is focused on short-term goals, and it is easily shattered when these are not realized. The quest for kicks, or mystical meaning, or celebration of life in the present moment, are, in part, an expression of the loss of hope, a loss we older people have bequeathed to our children. Is there, nevertheless, for us also a basis of hope somehow equivalent to that of the Bible?

I cannot speak here for all men, or for all religious men, or even for all Christians. But for myself the answer is "yes." The fact that when chemical conditions make it possible life appears, with growth and reproduction, means to me that there is that in reality that calls life forth and forward and strives against the forces of inertia and death. The fact that the human psyche is capable of being claimed by truth and touched by concern for fellow human beings means to me that there is that in reality that calls forth honesty and love and strives against the retreat into security, narrow interests, and merely habitual behavior. This power works slowly and quietly by persuasion without calling attention to itself. It does not present itself for observation by biologist or psychologist. Yet, it is presupposed in both the organism he studies and in his own faithful pursuit of truth. It is not to be found somewhere outside the organisms in which it is at work, but it is not to be identified with them either. We can conceive it best as Spirit.

It is the belief in this Spirit, the giver of life and love, that is the basis of hope. In spite of all the destructive forces man lets loose against life on this planet, the Spirit of Life is at work in ever new and unforeseeable ways, countering and circumventing the obstacles man puts in its path. In spite of my strong tendencies to complacency and despair, I experience the Spirit in myself as calling forth the realistic hope apart from which there is no hope, and I am confident that what I find in myself is occurring in others also.

Since what makes for life and love and hope is not simply the decision of one individual or another, but a Spirit that moves us all, I do not have to suppose that my own efforts are of great consequence in order to believe them to be worthwhile. I can recognize that they may even be futile or misdirected and still persist in them as long as no clearer light is given. For I see what I do as part of something much greater, something in which each person participates to whatever extent he sensitively responds to the insights and opportunities that come his way. Belief in the Spirit is belief that I am not alone. That in working for life and love in hope, I am working *with* something much greater than myself; that there are possibilities for the future that cannot be simply projected out of the past; that even my mistakes and failures may be woven into a healing pattern of which I am not now aware.

Belief in the Spirit is no ground for complacency. There is no guarantee that men will respond to the Spirit's promptings in sufficient numbers and with sufficient sensitivity to begin the healing of the planet. But there is the possibility. The future *can* be different from the past. Therefore there is hope. Where there is life, there *is* hope.

Now we have returned full circle. We asked whether all this talk of changing attitudes, developing a new consciousness, and belief in God was worthwhile when the practical tasks at hand are so urgent. Is it not perhaps too late? But when we turned to consider whether it is in fact too late, it seemed that if we have hope it may not be too late, but if we despair, then there is indeed no hope. And when we asked how such hope can endure, we found ourselves grounding it in belief in Spirit. That Spirit, of course, is the God of whom we have been speaking. It is because of God that it may not be too late.

Discussion Questions

1. What practical steps can we take to help solve the ecological problems?
2. In what ways could worship or liturgy shape our attitude toward the world more effectively, leading to a new vision and commitment?
3. What forms should Christian self-denial take in our time? Why?
4. Is it too late to bother about changing attitudes? Are there any reasons to be hopeful?

Bibliography

The Ecological Crisis

Borgstrom, George. *The Hungry Planet*. New York: The Macmillan Co., 1965; New York: Collier Books, 1967.

Carson, Rachel. *The Silent Spring*. Boston: Houghton Mifflin, 1962; New York: Fawcett World Library, Crest Books, 1970.

De Bell, Garrett, ed. *The Environmental Handbook*. New York: Ballantine Books, 1970. (Lynn White, Jr.'s essay, treated at length in Chapter 4, is reprinted in this book.)

Ehrlich, Paul. *The Population Bomb*. New York: Ballantine Books, 1968.

Forrester, Jay W. *World Dynamics*. Cambridge, Mass.: Wright–Allen Press, 1971.

Leopold, Aldo. *A Sand County Almanac*. New York: Oxford University Press, 1949; New York: Ballantine Books, 1970.

Marsh, George Perkins. *Man and Nature*. Edited by David Lowenthal. Cambridge, Mass.: Belknap Press of Harvard University Press, 1965.

Rienow, Robert and Leona. *Moment in the Sun*. New York: Ballantine Books, 1969.

Udall, Stewart. *The Quiet Crisis*. New York: Holt, Rinehart & Winston, 1964; New York: Avon Books, 1970.

Relevant Theological Writings

Christians and the Good Earth. Alexandria, Va.: Faith-Man-Nature Group, 1969.

Elder, Frederick. *Crisis in Eden*. New York: Abingdon Press, 1970.

Hamilton, Michael, ed. *The Little Planet*. New York: Charles Scribner's Sons, 1970.

Slusser, G. and D. M. *Technology: The God That Failed*. Philadelphia: Westminster Press, 1971.

Theological Books on Abortion and Contraception

American Friends Service Committee. *Who Shall Live?* New York: Hill & Wang, 1970.

Callahan, Daniel J. *Abortion: Law, Choice, and Morality*. New York: The Macmillan Co., 1970.

Noonan, John Thomas. *Contraception*. Cambridge, Mass.: Belknap Press of Harvard University Press, 1965.